C. H. SPURGEON

CHRISTIAN FESTIVALS

Sermons for Special Occasions

Lakeland

LAKELAND
BLUNDELL HOUSE
GOODWOOD ROAD
LONDON SE14 6BL

Previously published in *Sermons for Special Occasions*
(Kelvedon Edition)

This edition 1972

ISBN 0 551 00278 6

Printed in Great Britain by
Lowe & Brydone (Printers) Ltd., London

CONTENTS

1

THE NEW YEAR'S GUEST

"I was a stranger, and ye took me in."—Matthew 25: 35.
"But as many as received him, to them gave he power to become the sons of God, even to them that believe on his name."
—John 1: 12.

I LATELY received a New Year's card, which suggested to me the topic on which I am about to speak to you. The designer of the card has, with holy insight, seen the relation of the two texts to each other, and rendered both of them eminently suggestive by placing them together. There is freshness in the thought that, by receiving Jesus as a stranger, our believing hospitality works in us a divine capacity and we thereby receive power to become the sons of God. The connection suggested between the two inspired words is really existent, and by no means strained or fanciful, as you will see by reading the context of the passage in John: "He was in the world, and the world was made by him, and the world knew him not." So he was a stranger in the world which he himself had made. "He came unto his own, and his own received him not." So he was a stranger among the people whom he had set apart for his own by many deeds of mercy. "But as many as received him," —that is to say, gave entertainment to this blessed Stranger— "to them gave he power to become the sons of God, even to them that believe on his name."

I thought that this might prove to be a suitable and salutary passage to discourse upon at the beginning of a New Year, for this is a season of hospitality, and some among our friends will think it well to commence a New Year by saying to the Lord Jesus, "Come in, thou blessed of the Lord; wherefore standest thou without?" This divine stranger has knocked at many doors, till his head is wet with dew, and his locks with the drops of the night; and now I trust there are some who will rise up and open unto him, so that at the end of the year they may say with Job, "The stranger did not lodge in the street: but I opened my doors to the traveller." Verily, in so doing, you will not only entertain angels unawares; but you will be receiving the Lord of angels. The day in which you receive him shall be the beginning of years to you; it shall be the first of a series of years, which, whether they be few or many, shall be each one in the best sense *happy*.

I would say a few words, first, about *the Stranger taken in;* and then, about *the Stranger making strangers into sons.*

FIRST: THE STRANGER TAKEN IN: this is a simile given to us by our Lord himself: a royal metaphor presented to us from his own throne. Note that the passage begins, "I was an hungred, and ye gave me meat: I was thirsty, and ye gave me drink"; these are two good works which prove faith in Jesus and love to him, and therefore they are accepted, recorded, and rewarded; but it is a distinct and memorable growth when it comes to, "I was a Stranger, and ye took me in." House-room is a larger gift than refreshment at the door. It is good believingly to do anything for Christ, however small; but it is a much better thing to give entertainment to Jesus within our souls, admitting him into our minds and hearts. We have not come to the full of what our Lord has a right to expect of us till, having given from our stores to him, by benefiting his poor and aiding his cause, we deliberately open the doors of our entire being to him, and install him in our souls as an honoured guest. We must not be satisfied with giving him cups of cold water, or morsels of bread; but we must "constrain him, saying, Abide with us." Our hearts must be Bethanies, where, like Mary, and Martha, and Lazarus, we give our Master gladsome welcome: houses of Obed-edom, where the ark of the Lord may dwell in peace. Our prayer must be that of Abraham, "My Lord, if now I have found favour in thy sight, pass not away, I pray thee, from thy servant."

The uppermost word of our text is *stranger*, and its light casts a hue of strangeness over the whole passage. Here are three strange things. The first is, *that the Lord Jesus should be a Stranger here below*. Is it not a strange thing that "he was in the world, and the world was made by him," and yet he was a Stranger in it? Yet is it not a whit more strange than true; for when he was born there was no room for him in the inn. Inns had open doors for ordinary strangers, but not for him; for he was a greater stranger than any around him. It was Bethlehem of David, the seat of the ancient family to which he belonged; but alas! he had become "a stranger unto his brethren, and an alien unto his mother's children," and no door was open unto him. Soon there was no safe room for him in the village itself, for Herod the king sought the young child's life, and he must flee into Egypt, to be a Stranger in a strange land, and worse than a Stranger—an exile and a fugitive from the land whereof by birthright he was king. On his return, and on his public appearing, there was still no room for him among the mass of the people. He came to his own Israel, to whom prophets had revealed him, and types had set him forth; but they would have none of him. "He was despised and rejected of men." He was the man "whom men abhorred;" whom they so much detested that they cried, "Away with him! Crucify him!" Yea, the world so little knew him that they must needs hang up the Lord of glory on a cross, and put "the Holy One and the Just" to a felon's death. Jew and Gentile alike conspired to prove how truly he was a Stranger; the Jew said, "As for this fellow, we know not from whence he is;" and the Roman asked him, "Whence art thou?" Now, that Christ should be such a Stranger was indeed a sadly singular thing, and yet we need not wonder, for how should a wicked, selfish world know Jesus or receive him?

The Lord's own had been forewarned of this in ancient type, for long before the Lord appeared in the flesh he had shown himself as a stranger to the faithful. He came in angelic form to Abraham, and thus we read the story: "And he lift up his eyes and looked, and, lo, three men stood by him: and when he saw them, he ran to meet them from the tent door, and bowed himself toward the ground. And said, My Lord, if now I have found favour in thy sight, pass not away, I pray thee, from thy servant: Let a little water, I pray you, be fetched, and wash your feet, and rest yourselves under the tree: and I will fetch a morsel of bread, and comfort ye your hearts." The Lord, who stands out in the centre of the three, was a stranger, and the father of the faithful entertained him, in type of what all the faithful of every age will do. This is he of whom Jeremiah said, "O the hope of Israel, the Saviour thereof in time of trouble, why shouldest thou be as a stranger in the land, and as a wayfaring man that turneth aside to tarry for a night?" Yet with this fair warning it still remains sadly singular that, coming on an errand of mercy, our Lord should find so scant a welcome; should be so little known, so seldom recognized, so harshly entreated. Truly as Egypt made Israel to serve with rigour, so have we made this patient stranger to serve with our sins, and wearied him with our iniquities. The son of man had not where to lay his head. Luke says the barbarians showed Paul and his friends no little kindness: but men were worse than barbarians to their Saviour. Shall the servant be better treated than his Master, or the disciple than his Lord? "Behold, what manner of love the Father hath bestowed upon us, that we should be called the sons of God: therefore the world knoweth us not, because it knew him not."

Another strange thing is that *we should be able to receive the Lord Jesus as a Stranger.* He has gone into the glory, and will he ever say of us, "I was a stranger, and ye took me in"? Yes, he will say so, if we render to him that spiritual hospitality of which he here speaks. This can be done in several ways.

Brethren and sisters in Christ, for such I trust you are, we can receive Christ as a stranger when believers are few and despised in any place. We may sojourn where worldliness abounds and religion is at a discount, and it may need some courage to avow our faith in Jesus. Then have we an opportunity of winning the approving word, "I was a stranger, and ye took me in." There is a sure proof of love in receiving our Lord as a Stranger. If the Queen desired again to visit Mentone, every villa would be gladly placed at her disposal; but were she driven from her empire, and reduced to be a poor stranger, hospitality to her would be a greater test of loyalty than it is to-day. When Jesus is in low esteem in any place, and he sometimes is so, let us be all the more bold to avow our allegiance to him. I fear that many professors take their colour from their company, and are hail-fellows with the irreligious and the unbelieving. These cry "Hosanna" with the multitude of the Lord's admirers, but in heart they have no love to the Son of God. Our loyalty to Christ must never be a matter of latitude and longitude; we must love him in every land, honour him when the many disregard him, and we must speak of him when all forget him.

Again, we have the Lord's own warrant for saying that if we show brotherly kindness to a poor saint we entertain the Lord himself. If we see a sincere Christian in want, or despised, and ridiculed; and we say, "You are my brother; it matters not what garb you wear, the name of Christ is named on you, and I suffer with you. I will relieve your wants and share your reproach," then the glorious Lord himself will say to us at the last, "Inasmuch as ye have done it unto one of the least of these my brethren, ye have done it unto me." It does seem passing strange, though I thus speak, that you and I should be still able to entertain our Lord, and yet it is so. We do not wonder that the righteous with a humble truthfulness exclaim, "Lord, when saw we thee an hungred, and fed thee? or thirsty, and gave thee drink? When saw we thee a stranger, and took thee in?" Neither are we ourselves free from admiring surprise. We also cry, "Will God in very deed dwell with men upon the earth? Will he accept hospitality at our hands?" It is even so.

Again, we may entertain the stranger Christ by holding fast his faithful word when the doctrines taught by himself and his apostles are in ill repute. Nowadays the truth which God has revealed seems of less account with men than their own thoughts and dreams, and they who still believe Christ's faithful word shall have it said of them, "I was a stranger, and ye took me in." When you see revealed truth, as it were, wandering about in sheepskins and goatskins, being destitute, afflicted, tormented, and no man saith a good word for it, then is the hour come to avow it because it is Christ's truth, and to prove your fidelity by counting the reproach of Christ greater riches than all the treasures of Egypt. Oh! scorn on those who only believe what everybody else believes, just because they must be in the swim with the majority. These are but dead fish borne on the current, and they will be washed away to a shameful end. As living fish swim against the stream, so do living Christians pursue Christ's truth against the set and current of the times, defying alike the ignorance and the culture of the age. It is the believer's honour, the chivalry of a Christian, to be the steadfast friend of truth when all other men have forsaken it.

So, also, when Christ's precepts are disregarded, his day forgotten, and his worship neglected, we can come in, and take up our cross, and follow him, and so receive him as a Stranger. To be sure, some will say, "Those people are fanatical Methodists, or straitlaced Presbyterians;" but what of that? It matters nothing to us what the world thinks of us, for we are crucified to it and it to us. If our Lord has laid down a rule, it is ours to follow it, and find rest unto our souls in so doing; ay, and a special rest in doing it, when by so doing we are securing that blessed sentence, "I was a stranger, and ye took me in." Death itself for his sake would be a small matter if thereby we secured that priceless word.

Once more, that spiritual life, which is the innermost receiving of Christ; that new life, which no man knows but he that has received it; that quickening of the Spirit, which makes the Christian as much superior to ordinary men as men are above dumb, driven cattle—if we receive that blessed gift, then shall we with emphasis be entertaining our Lord as a Stranger. Profession is abundant, but the secret life is rare. The name to live is everywhere, but where is the life fully seen? To *be* rather than to talk, to *enjoy* rather than to pretend, to have Christ truly within—this is not every man's attainment, but those who have it are among the God-like ones, the true sons of God.

A third strange thing is the fact that *Jesus will deign to dwell in our hearts*. Such a one as Jesus in such a one as I am! The King of glory in a sinner's bosom! This is a miracle of grace: yet the manner of it is simple enough. A humble, repenting faith opens the door, and Jesus enters the heart at once. Love shuts to the door with the hand of penitence, and holy watchfulness keeps out intruders. Thus is the promise made good, "If any man hear my voice, and open the door, I will come in to him, and will sup with him, and he with me." Meditation, contemplation, prayer, praise, and daily obedience, keep the house in order for the Lord; and then follows the consecration of our entire nature to his use as a temple; the dedication of spirit, soul, and body, and all their powers, as holy vessels of the sanctuary; the writing of "Holiness unto the Lord" upon all that is about us, till our every-day garments become vestments, our meals sacraments, our life a ministry, and ourselves priests unto the Most High. Oh, the supreme condescension of this indwelling! He never dwelt in angel, but he resides in a contrite spirit. There is a world of meaning in the Redeemer's words, "I in them." May we know them as Paul translates them, "Christ in you, the hope of glory."

SECONDLY: THE STRANGER MAKING STRANGERS INTO SONS. "As many as received him, to them gave he power to become the sons of God, even to them that believe on his name." Yes, beloved, the moment Christ is received into our hearts by faith we are no more strangers and foreigners, but of the household of God; for the Lord *adopts us* and puts us among the children. It is a splendid act of divine grace, that he should take us who were heirs of wrath, and make us heirs of God, joint-heirs with Jesus Christ. Such honour have all the saints, even all that believe on his name.

There is more to follow: the designation of sons brings with it *a birth* into the actual condition of sons: the privilege brings with it the power, the name is backed up and warranted by the nature: for the Spirit of God enters into us when Christ comes, and causes us to be born again. To be adopted without being born again would be a lame blessing, but when we are both adopted and regenerated, then have we the fulness of son-ship, and the grace is made perfect towards us. "Except a man be born again, he cannot see the kingdom of God"; but this mysterious birth, which comes with the reception of Christ, makes us free, not only of the kingdom of God, but of the house and the heart of God.

Forget not that when the Lord Jesus enters our hearts, there springs up between us and him a living, loving, *lasting union*, and this seals our sonship: for as we become one with the Son we must be sons also. Jesus puts it, "My Father and your Father." It is the Spirit of his Son in our hearts by which we cry, "Abba, Father." "He that is joined unto the Lord is one spirit." We are unto the Father even as Jesus is, as he says "thou hast loved them as thou hast loved me." Thus you see that in receiving Jesus we receive, as the Revised Version puts it, "the right to become the sons of God."

Yet once more: the practical reception of Jesus into the life becomes a proof to ourselves and others that we are the sons of God, for *it creates in us a likeness to God* which is apparent and unquestionable. For although Jehovah, our God, be incomprehensible and infinite, and his glory is inconceivable in its splendour, yet this fact we know of him, that in his bosom lies his

Son, with whom he is always well-pleased. When we receive Jesus into our bosom, as one with us, and when our joy and delight are in him, we do in that matter become like to the Father. Having thus with the Father the same object of love and delight, we are brought into fellowship with him, and begin to walk in the light, as he is in the light.

Moreover, having received Jesus, as a Stranger, we feel a tenderness henceforth towards *all* strangers, for we see in their condition some resemblance to our own. We have love to all who like ourselves are strangers with God, and sojourners, as all our fathers were, and thus again we are made like to God, of whom it is written, "The Lord preserveth the strangers." Our God is "kind unto the unthankful and to the evil." Our Lord Jesus therefore bade us be the children of our Father which is in heaven, "For he maketh his sun to rise on the evil and on the good, and sendeth rain on the just and on the unjust." By becoming doers of good, we are known as children of the good God. "Blessed are the peacemakers: for they shall be called the children of God." A man is a son of God when he lives beyond himself by a thoughtful care for others; when his soul is not confined within the narrow circle of his own ribs, but goes abroad to bless those around him however unworthy they may be. True children of God never see a lost one without seeking to save him; never hear of misery without longing to bestow comfort. "Ye know the heart of a stranger," said the Lord to Israel; and so do we, for we were once captives ourselves, and even now our choicest Friend is still a Stranger, for whose sake we love all suffering men. When Christ is in us we search out opportunities of bringing prodigals, strangers, and outcasts to the great Father's house. Our love goes out to all mankind, and our hand is closed against none: if it be so we are made like to God, as little children are like their father. Oh! sweet result of entertaining the Son of God by faith: he dwells in us, and we gaze upon him in holy fellowship; so that "we all with open face beholding as in a glass the glory of the Lord, are changed into the same image, from glory to glory, even as by the Spirit of the Lord."

2

IMMEASURABLE LOVE

"For God so loved the world, that he gave his only begotten Son, that whosoever believeth in him should not perish, but have everlasting life."—John 3 : 16.

I WAS very greatly surprised the other day, in looking over the list of texts from which I have preached, to find that I have no record of ever having spoken from this verse. This is all the more singular, because I can truly say that it might be put in the forefront of all my volumes of discourses as the sole topic of my life's ministry. It has been my one and only business to set forth the love of God to men in Christ Jesus. I heard lately of an aged minister of whom it was said, "Whatever his text, he never failed to set forth God as love, and Christ as the atonement for sin." I wish that much the same may be said of me. My heart's desire has been to sound forth as with a trumpet the good news that "God so loved the world, that he gave his only begotten Son, that whosoever believeth in him should not perish, but have everlasting life."

We are about to meet around the communion table, and I cannot preach from this text anything but a simple gospel sermon. Can you desire a better preparation for communion? We have fellowship with God and with one another upon the basis of the infinite love which is displayed in Jesus Christ our Lord. The gospel is the fair white linen cloth which covers the table on which the Communion Feast is set. The higher truths, those truths which belong to a more enlightened experience, those richer truths which tell of the fellowship of the higher life—all these are helpful to holy fellowship; but I am sure not more so than those elementary and foundation truths which were the means of our first entrance into the kingdom of God. Babes in Christ and men in Christ here feed upon one common food. Come, aged saints, be children again;

and you that have long known your Lord, take up your first spelling book, and go over your A B C again, by learning that God so loved the world, that he gave his Son to die, that man might live through him.

To-night, we have to talk about the love of God: "God so loved the world." That love of God is a very wonderful thing, especially when we see it set upon a lost, ruined, guilty world. What was there in the world that God should love it? There was nothing lovable in it. No fragrant flower grew in that arid desert. Enmity to him, hatred to his truth, disregard of his law, rebellion against his commandments; those were the thorns and briars which covered the waste land; but no desirable thing blossomed there. Yet, "God loved the world," says the text; "so" loved it, that even the writer of the book of John could not tell us how much; but so greatly, so divinely, did he love it that he gave his Son, his only Son, to redeem the world from perishing, and to gather out of it a people to his praise.

Whence came that love? Not from anything outside of God himself. God's love springs from himself. He loves because it is his nature to do so. "God is love." As I have said already, nothing upon the face of the earth could have merited his love, though there was much to merit his displeasure. This stream of love flows from its own secret source in the eternal Deity, and it owes nothing to any earth-born rain or rivulet; it springs from beneath the everlasting throne, and fills itself full from the springs of the infinite. God loved because he would love. When we enquire why the Lord loved this man or that, we have to come back to our Saviour's answer to the question, "Even so, Father, for so it seemed good in thy sight." God has such love in his nature that he must needs let it flow forth to a world perishing by its own wilful sin; and when it flowed forth it was so deep, so wide, so strong, that even inspiration could not compute its measure, and therefore the Holy Spirit gave us that great little word SO, and left us to attempt the measurement, according as we perceive more and more of love divine.

Now, there happened to be an occasion upon which the great God could display his immeasurable love. The world had sadly gone astray; the world had lost itself; the world was tried and condemned; the world was given over to perish, because of its offences; and there was need for help. The fall of Adam and the destruction of mankind made ample room and verge enough for love almighty. Amid the ruins of humanity there was space for showing how much Jehovah loved the sons of men; for the compass of his love was no less than the world, the object of it no less than to deliver men from going down to the pit, and the result of it no less than the finding of a ransom for them. The far-reaching purpose of that love was both negative and positive; that, believing in Jesus, men might not perish, but have eternal life. The desperate disease of man gave occasion for the introduction of that divine remedy which God alone could have devised and supplied. By the plan of mercy, and the great gift which was needed for carrying it out, the Lord found means to display his boundless love to guilty men. Had there been no fall, and no perishing, God might have shown his love to us as he does to the pure and perfect spirits that surround his throne; but he never could have commended his love to us to such an extent as he now does. In the gift of his only-begotten Son, God commended his love to us, in that while we were yet sinners, in due time Christ died for the ungodly.

I might handle my text in a thousand different ways to-night; but for simplicity's sake, and to keep to the one point of setting forth the love of God, I want to make you see how great that love is by five different particulars.

The first is the GIFT: "God so loved the world, *that he gave his only begotten Son.*" Men who love much will give much, and you may usually measure the truth of love by its self-denials and sacrifices. That love which spares nothing, but spends itself to help and bless its object, is love indeed, and not the mere name of it. Little love forgets to bring water for the feet, but great love breaks its box of alabaster and lavishes its precious ointment.

Consider, then, *what this gift was* that God gave. I should have to labour for expression if I were to attempt to set forth to the full this priceless boon; and I will not court a failure by attempting the impossible. I will only invite you to think of the sacred Person whom the Great Father gave in order that he might prove his love to men. It was his only-begotten Son—his beloved Son, in whom he was well pleased. None of us had ever such a son to give. Ours are the sons of men; his was the Son of God. The Father gave his other self, one with himself.

When the great God gave his Son he gave God himself, for Jesus is not in his eternal nature less than God. When God gave God for us he gave himself. What more could he give? God gave his all: he gave himself. Who can measure this love?

Judge, ye fathers, how ye love your sons: could ye give them to die for your enemy? Judge, ye that have an only son, how your hearts are entwined about your first-born, your only-begotten. There was no higher proof of Abraham's love to God than when he did not withhold from God his son, his only son, his Isaac whom he loved; and there can certainly be no greater display of love than for the Eternal Father to give his only-begotten Son to die for us. No living thing will readily lose its offspring; man has peculiar grief when his son is taken; has not God yet more?

If you desire to see the love of God in this great procedure you must consider *how he gave his Son*. He did not give his Son, as you might do, to some profession in the pursuit of which you might still enjoy his company; but he gave his Son to exile among men. He sent him down to yonder manger, united with a perfect manhood, which at the first was in an infant's form. There he slept, where horned oxen fed! The Lord God sent the heir of all things to toil in a carpenter's shop: to drive the nail, and push the plane, and use the saw. He sent him down amongst scribes and Pharisees, whose cunning eyes watched him, and whose cruel tongues scourged him with base slanders. He sent him down to hunger, and thirst, amid poverty so dire that he had not where to lay his head. He sent him down to the scourging and the crowning with thorns, to the giving of his back to the smiters and his cheeks to those that plucked off the hair. At length he gave him up to death—a felon's death, the death of the crucified. Behold that cross and see the anguish of him that dies upon it, and mark how the Father has so given him, that he hides his face from him, and seems as if he would not own him! "Lama sabachthani" ("why hast Thou forsaken Me?") tells us how fully God gave his Son to ransom the souls of the sinful. He gave him to be made a curse for us; gave him that he might die "the just for the unjust, to bring us to God."

Dear sirs, I can understand your giving up your children to go to India on her Majesty's service, or to go out to the Cameroons or the Congo upon the errands of our Lord Jesus.

I can well comprehend your yielding them up even with the fear of a pestilential climate before you, for if they die they will die honourably in a glorious cause; but could you think of parting with them to die a felon's death, upon a gibbet, execrated by those whom they sought to bless, stripped naked in body and deserted in mind? Would not that be too much? Would you not cry, "I cannot part with my son for such wretches as these. Why should he be put to a cruel death for such abominable beings, who even wash their hands in the blood of their best friend"? Remember that our Lord Jesus died what his countrymen considered to be an accursed death. To the Romans it was the death of a condemned slave, a death which had all the elements of pain, disgrace, and scorn mingled in it to the uttermost. "But God commendeth his love toward us, in that, while we were yet sinners, Christ died for us." Oh, wondrous stretch of love, that Jesus Christ should die!

Yet, I cannot leave this point till I have you notice *when God gave his Son*, for there is love in the time. "God so loved the world that he gave his Only Begotten Son." But when did he do that? In his eternal purpose he did this from before the foundation of the world. The words here used, "He gave his Only Begotten Son," cannot relate exclusively to the death of Christ, for Christ was not dead at the time of the utterance of this third chapter of John. Our Lord had just been speaking with Nicodemus, and that conversation took place at the beginning of his ministry. The fact is that Jesus was always the gift of God. The promise of Jesus was made in the garden of Eden almost as soon as Adam fell. On the spot where our ruin was accomplished, a Deliverer was bestowed whose heel should be bruised, but who should break the serpent's head beneath his foot.

Throughout the ages the great Father stood to his gift. He looked upon his Only Begotten as man's hope, the inheritance of the chosen seed, who in him would possess all things. Every sacrifice was God's renewal of his gift of grace, a reassurance that he had bestowed the gift, and would never draw back therefrom. The whole system of types under the law betokened that in the fulness of time the Lord would in very deed give up his Son, to be born of a woman, to bear the iniquities of his people, and to die the death in their behalf. I greatly admire this pertinacity of love; for many a man in a moment of generous excitement can perform a supreme act of benevolence, and yet could not bear to look at it calmly, and consider it from year to year; the slow fire of anticipation would have been unbearable. If the Lord should take away yonder dear boy from his mother, she would bear the blow with some measure of patience, heavy as it would be to her tender heart; but suppose that she were credibly informed that on such a day her boy must die, and thus had from year to year to look upon him as one dead, would it not cast a cloud over every hour of her future life? Suppose also that she knew that he would be hanged upon a tree to die, as one condemned; would it not embitter her existence? If she could withdraw from such a trial, would she not? Assuredly she would. Yet the Lord God spared not his own Son, but freely delivered him up for us all, doing it in his heart from age to age. Herein is love: love which many waters could not quench: love eternal, inconceivable, infinite!

Now, as this gift refers not only to our Lord's death, but to the ages before it, so it includes also all the ages afterwards. God "so loved the world that he gave"—and still gives—"his only begotten Son, that whosoever believeth in him should not perish, but have everlasting life." The Lord is giving Christ away to-night. Oh, that thousands of you may gladly accept the gift unspeakable! Will anyone refuse? This good gift, this perfect gift,—can you decline it? Oh, that you may have faith to lay hold on Jesus, for thus he will be yours. He is God's free gift to all free receivers; a full Christ for empty sinners. If you can but hold out your empty willing hand, the Lord will give Christ to you at this moment. Nothing is freer than a gift. Nothing is more worth having than a gift which comes fresh from the hand of God, as full of effectual power as ever it was. The fountain is eternal, but the stream from it is as fresh as when first the fountain was opened. There is no exhausting this gift.

> *Dear dying Lamb, thy precious blood*
> *Shall never lose its power*
> *Till all the ransomed church of God*
> *Be saved to sin no more.*

I call upon you from this first point to admire the love of God, because of the transcendent greatness of his gift to the world, even the gift of his only begotten Son. Now notice secondly, and, I think I may say, with equal admiration, the love of God in THE PLAN OF SALVATION. He has put it thus: "that whosoever believeth on him should not perish, but have everlasting life." The way of salvation is extremely simple to understand, and exceedingly easy to practise, when once the heart is made willing and obedient. The method of the covenant of grace differs as much from that of the covenant of works as light from darkness. It is not said that God has given his Son to all who will keep his law, for that we could not do, and therefore the gift would have been available to none of us. Nor is it said that he has given his Son to all that experience terrible despair and bitter remorse, for that is not felt by many who nevertheless are the Lord's own people. But the great God has given his own Son, that "whosoever believeth in him" should not perish. Faith, however slender, saves the soul. Trust in Christ is the certain way of eternal happiness.

Now, what is it to believe in Jesus? It is just this: it is to trust yourself with him. If your hearts are ready, though you have never believed in Jesus before, I trust you will believe in him now. O Holy Spirit, graciously make it so.

What is it to believe in Jesus?

It is, first, to give your *firm and cordial assent* to the truth, that God did send his Son, born of a woman, to stand in the room and stead of guilty men, and that God did cause to meet on him the iniquities of us all, so that he bore the punishment due to our transgressions, being made a curse for us. We must heartily believe the Scripture which saith,—"the chastisement of our peace was upon him; and with his stripes we are healed." I ask for your assent to the grand doctrine of substitution, which is the marrow of the gospel. Oh, may God the Holy Spirit lead you to give a cordial assent to it at once; for wonderful as it is, it is a fact that God was in Christ reconciling the world unto himself, not imputing their trespasses upon them. Oh that you may rejoice that this is true, and be thankful that such a blessed fact is revealed by God himself. Believe that the substitution of the Son of God is certain; cavil not at the plan, nor question its validity, or efficacy, as many do. Alas! they kick at God's great sacrifice, and count it a sorry invention. As for me, since God has ordained to save man by a substitutionary sacrifice, I joyfully agree to his method, and see no reason to do anything else but admire it and adore the Author of it. I rejoice that such a plan should have been thought of, whereby the justice of God is vindicated, and his mercy is set free to do all that he desires. Sin is punished in the person of the Christ, yet mercy is extended to the guilty. In Christ mercy is sustained by justice, and justice satisfied by an act of mercy. The worldly wise say hard things about this device of infinite wisdom; but as for me, I love the very name of the cross, and count it to be the centre of wisdom, the focus of love, the heart of righteousness.

The second thing is that you do *accept this for yourself.* In Adam's sin, you did not sin personally, for you were not then in existence; yet you fell; neither can you now complain thereof, for you have willingly endorsed and adopted Adam's sin by committing personal transgressions. You have laid your hand, as it were, upon Adam's sin, and made it your own, by committing personal and actual sin. Thus you perished by the sin of another, which you adopted and endorsed; and in like manner must you be saved by the righteousness of another, which you are to accept and appropriate. Jesus has offered an atonement, and that atonement becomes yours when you accept it by putting your trust in him. I want you now to say,

> *My faith doth lay her hand*
> *On that dear head of thine,*
> *While, like a penitent, I stand,*
> *And here confess my sin.*

Surely this is no very difficult matter. To say that Christ who hung upon the cross shall be my Christ, my surety, needs neither stretch of intellect, nor splendour of character; and yet it is the act which brings salvation to the soul.

One thing more is needful; and that is *personal trust.* First comes assent to the truth, then acceptance of that truth for yourself, and then a simple trusting of yourself wholly to Christ, as a Substitute. The essence of faith is trust, reliance, dependence. Fling away every other confidence of every sort, save confidence in Jesus. Do not allow a ghost of a shade of a shadow of a confidence in anything that you can do, or in anything that you can be; but look alone to him whom God has set forth to be the propitiation for sin. This I do at this very moment; will you not do the same? Oh, may the sweet Spirit of God lead you now to trust in Jesus!

See, then, the love of God in putting it in so plain, so easy a way. Oh, broken, crushed and despairing sinner, thou canst not work, but canst thou not believe that which is true? Thou canst not sigh; thou canst not cry; thou canst not melt thy stony heart; but canst thou not believe that Jesus died for thee, and that he can change that heart of thine and make thee a new creature? If thou canst believe this, then trust in Jesus to do so, and thou art saved; for he that believes in him is justified. "He that believeth in him *hath* everlasting life." He is a saved man. His sins are forgiven him. Let him go his way in peace, and sin no more.

I admire, first, the love of God in the great gift, and then in the great plan by which that gift becomes available to guilty men. Thirdly, the love of God shines forth with transcendent brightness in a third point, namely, in THE PERSONS FOR WHOM THIS PLAN IS AVAILABLE, and for whom this gift is given. They are described in these words—"Whosoever believeth in him." There is in the text a word which has no limit—"God so loved the world"; but then comes in the descriptive limit, which I beg you to notice with care: "He gave his Only Begotten Son *that whosoever believeth in him* should not perish." God did not so love the world that any man who does not believe in Christ shall be saved; neither did God so give his Son that any man shall be saved who refuses to believe in him. See how it is put—"God so loved the world, that he gave his only begotten Son, that whosoever believeth in him should not perish." Here is the compass of the love: while every unbeliever is excluded, every believer is included. "Whosoever believeth in him." Suppose there be a man who has been guilty of all the lusts of the flesh to an infamous degree, suppose that he is so detestable that he is only fit to be treated like a moral leper, and shut up in a separate house for fear he should contaminate those who hear or see him; yet if that man shall believe in Jesus Christ, he shall at once be made clean from his defilement, and shall not perish because of his sin. And suppose there be another man who, in the pursuit of his selfish motives, has ground down the poor, has robbed his fellow-traders, and has even gone so far as to commit actual crime of which the law has taken cognisance, yet if he believes in the Lord Jesus Christ he shall be led to make restitution, and his sins shall be forgiven him.

I once heard of a preacher addressing a company of men in chains, condemned to die for murder and other crimes. They were such a drove of beasts to all outward appearances that it seemed hopeless to preach to them; yet were I set to be chaplain to such a wretched company I should not hesitate to tell them that "God so loved the world, that he gave his Only Begotten Son, that *whosoever* believeth in him should not perish, but have everlasting life." O man, if thou wilt believe in Jesus as the Christ, however horrible thy past sins have been they shall be blotted out; thou shalt be saved from the power of thine evil habits; and thou shalt begin again like a child new-born, with a new and true life, which God shall give thee. "Whosoever believeth in him,"—that takes you in, my agèd friend, now lingering within a few tottering steps of the grave. O grey-headed sinner, if you believe in him, you shall not perish. The text also includes you, dear boy, who have scarcely entered your teens as yet: if you believe in him, you shall not perish. That takes you in, fair maiden, and gives you hope and joy while yet young. That comprehends all of us, provided we believe in the Lord Jesus Christ. Neither can all the devils in hell find out any reason why the man that believes in Christ shall be lost, for it is written, "Him that cometh to me I will in no wise cast out."

Do they say, "Lord, he has been so long in coming"? The Lord replies,—"Has he come? Then I will not cast him out for all his delays." But, Lord, he went back after making a profession. "Has he at length come? Then I will not cast him out for all his backslidings." But, Lord, he was a foul-mouthed blasphemer. "Has he come to me? Then I will not cast him out for all his blasphemies." But, says one, "I take exception to the salvation of this wicked wretch. He has behaved so abominably that in all justice he ought to be sent to hell." Just so. But if he repents of his sin and believes in the Lord Jesus Christ, whoever he may be, he shall not be sent there. He shall be changed in character, so that he shall never perish, but have eternal life.

Now, observe, that this "whosoever" makes a grand sweep; for it encircles all degrees of faith. "Whosoever believeth in him." It may be that he has no full assurance; it may be that he has no assurance at all; but if he has faith, true and childlike, by it he shall be saved. Though his faith be so little that I must needs put on my spectacles to see it, yet Christ will see it and reward it. His faith is such a tiny grain of mustard seed that I look and look again but hardly discern it, and yet it brings him eternal life, and it is itself a living thing. The Lord can see within that mustard seed a tree among whose branches the birds of the air shall make their nests.

> *My faith is feeble, I confess,*
> *I faintly trust thy word;*
> *But wilt thou pity me the less?*
> *Be that far from thee, Lord!*

O Lord Jesus, if I cannot take thee up in my arms as Simeon did, I will at least touch thy garment's hem as the poor diseased woman did to whom thy healing virtue flowed. It is written, "God so loved the world that he gave his Only Begotten Son, that whosoever believeth in him should not perish, but have everlasting life." That means me. Oh that this truth may soak into your souls. Oh you that feel yourselves guilty; and you that feel guilty because you do not feel guilty; you that are broken in heart because your heart will not break; you that feel that you cannot feel; it is to you that I would preach salvation in Christ by faith. You groan because you cannot groan; but whoever you may be, you are still within the range of this mighty word, that "whosoever believeth in Him should not perish, but have eternal life."

Thus have I commended God's love to you in those three points—the divine gift, the divine method of saving, and the divine choice of the persons to whom salvation comes. Now fourthly, another beam of divine love is to be seen in the negative blessing here stated, namely, in THE DELIVERANCE implied in the words, "that whosoever believeth in him should *not perish.*"

25

I understand that word to mean that whosoever believes in the Lord Jesus Christ shall not perish, though he is ready to perish. His sins would cause him to perish, but he shall never perish. At first he has a little hope in Christ, but its existence is feeble. It will soon die out, will it not? No, his faith shall not perish, for this promise covers it—"Whosoever believeth in Him should not perish." The penitent has believed in Jesus, and therefore he has begun to be a Christian; "Oh," cries an enemy, "let him alone: he will soon be back among us; he will soon be as careless as ever." Listen. "Whosoever believeth in Him should not perish," and therefore he will not return to his former state. This proves the final perseverance of the saints; for if the believer ceased to be a believer he would perish; and as he cannot perish, it is clear that he will continue a believer. If thou believest in Jesus, thou shalt never leave off believing in him; for that would be to perish. If thou believest in him, thou shalt never delight in thine old sins; for that would be to perish. If thou believest in him, thou shalt never lose spiritual life. How canst thou lose that which is ever-lasting? If thou wert to lose it, it would prove that it was not everlasting, and thou wouldst perish; and thus thou wouldst make this word to be of no effect. Whosoever with his heart believeth in Christ is a saved man, not for to-night only, but for all the nights that ever shall be, and for that dread night of death, and for that solemn eternity which draws so near.

What is it to perish? It is to lose all hope in Christ, all trust in God, all light in life, all peace in death, all joy, all bliss, all union with God. This shall never happen to thee if thou believest in Christ. If thou believest, thou shalt be chastened when thou dost wrong, for every child of God comes under discipline; and what son is there whom the Father chasteneth not? If thou believest, thou mayest doubt and fear as to thy state, as a man on board a ship may be tossed about; but thou hast gotten on board a ship that never can be wrecked. He that hath union with Christ hath union with perfection, omnipotence and glory. He that believeth is a member of Christ: will Christ lose his members? How should Christ be perfect if he lost even his little finger? Are Christ's members to rot off, or to be cut off? Impossible. If thou hast faith in Christ thou art a partaker of Christ's life, and thou canst not

26

perish. If men were trying to drown me, they could not drown my foot as long as I had my head above water; and as long as our Head is above water, up yonder in the eternal sunshine, the least limb of his body can never be destroyed. He that believeth in Jesus is united to him, and he must live because Jesus lives. I do not believe that the man who is once in Christ may live in sin and delight in it, and yet be saved. That is abominable teaching, and none of mine. But I believe that the man who is in Christ will *not* live in sin, for he is saved from it; nor will he return to his old sins and abide in them, for the grace of God will continue to save him from his sins. It would be as great a miracle to undo the work of God as to do it; and to destroy the new creation would require as great a power as to make it. As only God can create, so only God can destroy; and he will never destroy the work of his own hands.

The last commendation of his love lies in *the positive*—IN THE POSSESSION. I shall have to go in a measure over the same ground again. Let me therefore be the shorter. God gives to every man that believes in Christ everlasting life. The moment thou believest there trembles into thy bosom a vital spark of heavenly flame which never shall be quenched. In that same moment when thou dost cast thyself on Christ, Christ comes to thee in the living and incorruptible word which liveth and abideth for ever. Though there should drop into thy heart but one drop of the heavenly water of life, remember this,—he hath said it who cannot lie,—"The water that I shall give him shall be in him a well of water springing up into everlasting life." When I first received everlasting life I had no idea what a treasure had come to me. I knew that I had obtained something very extraordinary, but of its superlative value I was not aware. I did but look to Christ in the little chapel, and I received eternal life. I looked to Jesus, and he looked on me: and we were one for ever. That moment my joy surpassed all bounds, just as my sorrow had aforetime driven me to an extreme of grief. I was perfectly at rest in Christ, satisfied with him, and my heart was glad; but I did not know that this grace was everlasting life till I began to read in the Scriptures, and to know more fully the value of the jewel which God had given me. The next Sunday I went to the same chapel, as it was very natural that I should. But I never went afterwards, for this reason, that during my first week the new life that was in me had been compelled to fight for its existence, and a conflict with the old nature had been vigorously carried on. This I knew to be a special token of the indwelling of grace in my soul; but in that same chapel I heard a sermon upon "O wretched man that I am! who shall deliver me from the body of this death?" And the preacher declared that Paul was not a Christian when he had that experience. Babe as I was, I knew better than to believe so absurd a statement. What but divine grace could produce such a sighing and crying after deliverance from indwelling sin? I felt that a person who could talk such nonsense knew little of the life of a true believer. I said to myself, "What! am I not alive because I feel a conflict within me? I never felt this fight when I was an unbeliever. When I was not a Christian I never groaned to be set free from sin." This conflict is one of the surest evidences of my new birth, the struggle becomes more and more intense; each victory over sin reveals another army of evil tendencies, and I am never able to sheathe my sword, nor cease from prayer and watchfulness.

I cannot advance an inch without praying my way, nor keep the inch I gain without watching and standing fast. Grace alone can preserve and perfect me. The old nature will kill the new nature if it can; and to this moment the only reason why my new nature is not dead is this—because it cannot die. If it could have died, it would have been slain long ago; but Jesus said, "I give unto my sheep eternal life"; "he that believeth on me hath everlasting life"; and therefore the believer cannot die. The only religion which will save you is one that you cannot leave, because it possesses you, and will not leave you. To have Christ living in you, and the truth ingrained in your very nature—O sirs, *this* is the thing that saves the soul, and nothing short of it. It is written in the text, "God so loved the world that he gave his only begotten Son, that whosoever believeth in him should not perish, but have everlasting life." What is this but a life that shall last through your three-score years and ten; a life that will out-shine those stars and yon sun and moon; a life that shall be co-eval with the life of the Eternal Father? As long as there is a God, the believer shall not only exist, but live.

3

· BONDS WHICH COULD NOT HOLD

"Whom God hath raised up, having loosed the pains of
death: because it was not possible that he should be holden
of it."—Acts 2: 24.

PETER is here speaking of the risen Christ, whom God had
raised up, "having loosed the pains of death;" so it is clear
that, whatever those pains were, our blessed Lord Jesus Christ
felt them, he felt them much more than his followers do; for,
in his death-agony, he was left without the sustaining help of
God, and the light of his Father's countenance was hidden from
him. His death was a bitter one indeed, he took the deepest
draughts of wormwood and gall, for he had to "taste death for
every man," whatever that mysterious expression may mean.
We must never imagine that there was about Christ's death
anything which took away from its bitterness; there was much
that increased it, but nothing that diminished it. He was bound,
as with strong cords, by the pains of death; all his powers were,
for a time, fettered, he was held captive, and he did really die.
After death, he was buried; but there was this remarkable
fact about his dead body, it saw no corruption. In the case of
ordinary corpses, corruption begins very speedily. In a climate
like that of Jerusalem, it is very quick in doing its work of
dissolving the mortal fabric; but, although our Lord did truly
die, no taint of corruption came upon his precious body.

The reason for that was, first, because it was not necessary.
Corruption is not a part of the sentence which Christ had to
bear. The penalty of sin is death, and that he bore to the
utmost; but there was no necessity that he should also endure
the usual consequences of death; and, therefore, although he
died, his flesh was not permitted to see corruption.

Again, as it was not necessary, so it would not have been
seemly that our Lord Jesus Christ's body should ever be tainted
by decay as all other bodies are. It was not right that One who

was so pure and holy as he was, One who stood in what theologians call hypostatical union with the Godhead (it is not easy to explain exactly what is meant by that term, but it refers to our Lord's intimate and complete union with the Godhead), it would not have been comely that such a body as his should see corruption, and, therefore, it was preserved from the defilement which death usually brings in its train.

And, further, it was not even natural that the body of Christ should see corruption, for albeit that it was like our bodies in many respects, yet we must never forget that there was a vast difference even in his birth. Through the immaculate conception of our Lord, no taint of sin was in his nature; by a mysterious overshadowing which we must not attempt to understand, "that holy thing" which was born of the virgin was truly "the Son of God," "holy, harmless, undefiled, separate from sinners"; and, as there was no original taint about that sacred body, so there was never afterwards a single action, or even thought, by which its chaste and perfect purity could have been defiled. If our first parents had never sinned, it would not have been necessary for these bodies of ours to die, and to become corrupt; and in taking our place, and suffering in our stead, there did come upon Christ the necessity that he should die, but there was no natural necessity that his dead body should become corrupt, and it did not pass into a state of decay, for it was not the will of God that his soul should be left in Hades, or that his holy body should see corruption. While it is quite true that Christ is made in all things like unto his brethren, yet there is always some point of distinction to indicate that, although he is our Brother, he is "the firstborn among many brethren," "the chiefest among ten thousand"; and, if others are lovely, yet "he is altogether lovely." So, although he really died, and his body was laid in the tomb as the dead usually are, yet, inasmuch as it was preserved from corruption, it is marked out as being above and different from all the rest.

I am going now to speak upon the fact mentioned in the text, that IT WAS NOT POSSIBLE THAT THE BONDS OF DEATH SHOULD HOLD OUR LORD. God raised him up, "having loosed the pains of death: because it was not possible that he should be holden of it."

Why was it impossible that the bonds of death should hold Christ? There are several reasons; the first is, that *Christ had in himself the inherent power to die, and to live again.* I will not enlarge upon this truth, but simply give you our Lord's own words concerning it: "Therefore doth my Father love me, because I lay down my life, that I might take it again. No man taketh it from me, but I lay it down of myself. I have power to lay it down, and I have power to take it again. This commandment have I received of my Father." Now, in the realms of the dead, before that time, there had never been seen any person who had the inherent power to take up his life again. Neither had there ever been one there who had possessed the inherent power to lay down his life when he pleased, for no mere man has ever been the absolute master of his own life; so that our Lord Jesus was the first who ever entered the portals of the tomb bearing within himself the power to rise again whenever he pleased.

Next, *the dignity of his person* rendered it impossible that he should be held by the cords of death, apart from the consent of his own will; for, though Jesus Christ was truly human,—and let that blessed fact never be forgotten,—yet his humanity was in so close an alliance with the Godhead, that, though we do not say that the humanity did really become divine, yet "Jesus Christ himself" altogether is divine, and is to be worshipped and adored in the completeness of his blessed Person; and, therefore, that flesh, which he took upon himself for our sake, was uplifted, exalted, ennobled, by being taken into mysterious unity with his Deity. It could not be that a body, in which dwelt the fullness of the Godhead, could be held by the bones of death. He who slept in Joseph's tomb was the Son of God. It was he who is without beginning of days or end of years, he with whom Jehovah took counsel when he laid the foundations of the heavens and built all worlds, for "without him was not anything made that was made." It was not, therefore, possible that he should be held by the bonds of death. Marvellous condescension, not human weakness, brought him into the sepulchre; it was by his own free will that he was laid in the tomb; and, consequently, he had but to exert his royal prerogative, and he could rise again from the dead whenever he pleased.

Those two reasons might be sufficient to prove the assertion I made concerning our Lord, but I want you to notice, with delight, a third one. It was not possible that the dead Christ should be held by the bonds of death any longer than the third morning *because his redeeming work was done.* Remember—and oh! how well some of you know it, and how gladly do you welcome it!—that the reason why Jesus died was because he took the sin of his people upon himself; and being found in the sinner's place, he had to suffer the sinner's doom, which was death. But after he had endured the penalty, that is, after he had died, and remained the appointed time in the tomb, how could he be held any longer in the grave? After he had said, "It is finished," and after the predestinated hours for a full examination of his work before the throne of God had passed, why should he be detained any longer? He was the Hostage for our debt; but when the debt was paid, who could keep him in durance vile? Having borne the penalty, he was free for ever; and so, as Paul writes, "Christ being raised from the dead dieth no more; death hath no more dominion over him." In that he has satisfied all the claims of the law of God, what hand can arrest him, what power can hold him captive? He died for our sins, but he rose again for our justification, and his rising proved that all his people were accounted righteous in the sight of God. It was not possible, while there was a just God in heaven, that Christ should remain in the tomb. As his work was done, justice demanded that he should be let go;—"And now both the Surety and sinner are free."

In the next place, it was not possible that Christ should remain in the tomb because *he had his Father's promise that he should not.* I have already reminded you that David, speaking by inspiration, had said, "Thou wilt not leave my soul in Hades" (the abode of departed spirits); "neither wilt thou suffer thine Holy One to see corruption." That promise must be kept, so it was not possible that Christ should remain in the grave beyond the appointed period; indeed, this was part of the Father's purpose and plan, and an essential part of the great work of the redemption of his elect, that he who died should rise again; and what is in Jehovah's plan and purpose, none shall ever gainsay. When he openeth the door, no man is able to shut it; and while he shutteth up, no man can possibly open.

Even Nebuchadnezzar, when he came to his right mind, said concerning the Most High, "None can stay his hand, or say unto him, What doest thou?" So, when the Father had purposed and decreed that his Son, Jesus Christ, should not be held any longer by the bonds of death, it was not possible for him to be detained.

Remember, too, that there is a fifth reason for Christ's deliverance; that is to be found in *the perpetuity of his offices.* You scarcely need for me to remind you that our Lord Jesus Christ was a Priest, but not after the order of the Aaronic priests, for they died, and there was an end of them so far as their priesthood was concerned; but to Christ it was said, "Thou art a priest for ever after the order of Melchisedec." But a man cannot be a priest when he is dead; therefore, since Christ's is a Melchisedec priesthood, he "is made, not after the law of a carnal commandment, but after the power of an endless life"; and, in order that he might have that endless life, it was necessary that he should rise from the dead,—his Melchisedec priesthood required it.

Next, Jesus was King as well as Priest. You know what sort of a King he was, for it is written, "Thy throne, O God, is for ever and ever." Now Christ must reign. It is also written that "he must reign, till he hath put all enemies under his feet." But a dead king cannot reign; and, therefore, Christ must rise from the tomb. He must have death under his feet, for death is one of his enemies; but if he had not risen from the dead, he would have been under the feet of death, and that could never be. So that both his priestly and kingly offices required that he should rise from the grave.

Ay, and so did his office as our Redeemer; for, when he undertook to become our next of kin, and to redeem us, it was essential that he should continue to live, or else that ancient cry of the patriarch Job would not have remained true, "I know that my Redeemer liveth." Therefore, he must rise from the dead. I cannot stay to go further into this argument; but, if you will think over it yourself, you will see that, because Jesus Christ is "the same yesterday, and to-day, and for ever," because each of his offices is everlasting, ordained of God in perpetuity, therefore he must rise from the dead.

But it was not possible, *in the very nature of things,* for Christ to be held by the bonds of death. If he had been, think what the consequences to us would have been; for, first, we should have had no assurance of our own resurrection. The blessed hope that those who have been called away from us, and whose bodies we have committed to the earth, shall rise again, would have been without any substantial foundation. "But now is Christ risen from the dead, and become the firstfruits of them that slept." When you get the firstfruits of a harvest, you feel certain that the rest of it will be garnered in due time. So Christ has risen as the first of a great host, and we thus have an assurance, which otherwise we could not have had, but which is essential to the comfort of Christians.

Only imagine what would have been the consequences to us if that assurance had not been ours. There would have been no evidence of our justification. I might have said, "Yes, Christ took my debt, but how do I know that he paid it? Christ bore my sins, but how do I know that he put them away?" So, if he had never risen from the dead, we should have had no proof that we were justified.

Then, too, if he had never risen, and gone up to heaven in his human body, we should not have had anyone to take possession of heaven on our behalf. Now we have "a man in possession." We have a wondrous Representative before the throne, who has taken seizin and grip of the divine estates. What a joy it is to us to know that he is there to represent us before God!

Further, if Christ's body had remained in the grave, there could have been no reign of Christ, and no sitting down at the right hand of God, as there now is. He would have been in heaven in the same respect as he is here as God; but there would have been no visible appearance of the representative Man, and the once-crucified Redeemer; and the ransomed ones could not have sung, "For thou wast slain, and hast redeemed us to God by thy blood," for he would not have been there to hear the song. They might have recollected the sacrifice on Calvary; but he, as the Lamb that had been slain, wearing the marks of his priesthood and death, would not have been there.

Now I pass on to my second observation, which is that, AS CHRIST COULD NOT BE HELD BY THE BONDS OF DEATH, HE COULD NOT BE HELD BY ANY OTHER BONDS.

If he was more than a match for death, who or what shall ever be able to stand against him? Death, the slaughterer of all mankind, before whom kings and princes, as well as the meanest of their subjects, lie prostrate in the tomb—death, before whom giants bend as a rush sways to and fro in the wind—; even death is vanquished by Christ. He is the destroyer of destruction, and the death of death; then, what power can possibly stand in opposition to him? I want to cheer you, in these dark and evil days, with a strong belief in our great Master's omnipotence and invincible might. His kingdom is an everlasting kingdom. With such a Hero as he is to lead us on, victory is sure, however stern may be the conflict.

Think, for a few minutes, how many things have tried to bind the Christ of God, and to overthrow his righteous rule. At first, and even until now, *old-established error* has assailed the truth of God. What fools some people thought that those few fishermen were when they imagined that they could upset the firmly-established Judaism of the chosen people and the deeply-ingrained idolatry of other nations! The systems of the heathen were beautiful with art, adorned with poetry, intensely lascivious, and they had a tremendous power over the popular mind. If we had lived in those days, and had been unbelievers who had seen those fishermen start out to preach, we should have said to them, "Go home with you! Do you think you are ever going to overthrow the philosophies of Plato and Socrates, and all the reverence for the gods and goddesses of Greece and Rome?" Ah! but from their deep foundations that little band of men plucked up by the very roots those old idolatries, for Christ could not be held in bondage by them.

Then there came another period, in which men thought themselves exceedingly wise, and *the wisdom of this world* set itself in array against the gospel of Christ, even as it does to-day; but he who was Victor over death can never be defeated by the Academy. Think not, beloved, that the most learnèd fools can be a match for him who overcame death itself. When Christ's cause was at the lowest ebb, when he himself was dead, and all his disciples were scattered, yet even then he snatched the crown from the hands of the skeleton king, and won a complete victory over him. Think you that he, who is Wisdom Incarnate, does not know how the wise men and the scribes

35

of to-day jest and jeer at him? Yet there is no philosopher who can bind the Christ any more than Samson could be bound by the green withs of the Philistines.

Next, there came a time when men tried to bind up the kingdom of Christ with *the bonds of ignorance.* They took away the Bible from the people, they concealed the gospel in the Latin tongue, and the nations were steeped in midnight darkness. Yet Christ could not be bound even then. He had only to call Wycliffe, and Huss, and Jerome, and Luther, and Calvin, and Melanchthon, and Zwingli, and very soon they let men know that Christ could not be held in the bonds of the Pope. The Conqueror of death was not to be vanquished by any mortal man, whoever he might be.

Since then, we have come to times in which *wealth, and rank, and fashion, and prestige,* are all against the gospel; but what matters it? Nowadays, the multitudes pour their scorn upon righteousness, and call that "cant and hypocrisy" which is really a defence of that which is right and true; and Satan is casting a fatal spell over the professing church itself, so that it is getting worldly, and is giving up its primitive simplicity. Sometimes, I am inclined to sit down and weep and grieve, as I see how sadly the battle seems to go against us today; we seem to be losing ground, instead of gaining the victory. But will I wring my hands in despair? God forbid! "The Strength of Israel will not lie," neither shall his cause fail. Let men forsake him if they will, or let them come out armed against him if they dare, his kingdom shall still stand fast, for he must reign, and, as death cannot bind him, nothing else can. The pleasure of the Lord must prosper in his hands, therefore in patience possess your souls; go on quietly witnessing for Christ; and, if you do not see the rulers of the nations converted to Christ, and the great and learned men bowing humbly before him, remember that it was never so, and is never likely to be so. Take care that you yourselves remain steadfast in faith in the Eternal, and all shall be well with you.

Now, there is a truth upon which I wish to insist with great earnestness; it is this. AS CHRIST COULD NOT BE HELD BY THE BONDS OF DEATH, IT IS NOT POSSIBLE TO KEEP IN BONDAGE ANYTHING THAT BELONGS TO HIM.

You recollect that, when Pharaoh told Moses that the men

among the children of Israel might go into the wilderness to offer sacrifice, he said that they must leave their little ones behind; but Moses would not accept that condition. The next time, Pharaoh said, "Go ye, serve the Lord; only let your flocks and your herds be stayed: let your little ones also go with you." But Moses answered, "Thou must give us also sacrifices and burnt offerings, that we may sacrifice unto the Lord our God. Our cattle also shall go with us; there shall not an hoof be left behind" (Exod. 10: 24-26). All that was of Israel was to go with Israel; and that is still our Master's will and way. "Where I am," saith he, "there shall my people be also. If I am in the grave, they must be in the grave, too, buried with me; if I rise, they also shall rise, for I will not rise without them; and, if I go to heaven, I will not go without them." This is our joy, and with dear old Rowland Hill we can sing,—

> *And this do I find, we two are so joined,*
> *He'll not be in glory, and leave me behind.*

Now, where are you, *you who are struggling to get to Christ?* You are somewhere in this place, I verily believe. You have been resolving to find Christ, and you have really put your trust in him; it is a very poor little trust as yet, and no sooner have you begun to think seriously about divine things, than you are in great trouble. There are your old sins, and you wonder how you will ever get rid of the guilt of former years. Ah! if you fully trust in Christ, your old sins shall vanish away through his precious blood. They are bonds that cannot hold a soul for whom Christ hath died. "Oh, but there are also my old habits," says one, "my tendency to do what I have been doing for years. 'Can the Ethiopian change his skin, or the leopard his spots?' How then shall I, who have been accustomed to do evil, learn to do well?" Put you your trust in Christ, and those old habits shall not be able to hold you. They may, perhaps, take some time to break; but they shall all be broken, and you shall be set free. Christ could not be held by the bonds of death, neither shall you, who truly trust him, be held by the bonds of habit. Possibly you say, "My old companions get round me, and they worry me to go back to them." Let them worry as much as they like; but, if you trust in Christ,

God will give you grace to set your face like a flint against them, and you shall be a bolder and braver soldier of Christ because they oppose you. Perhaps it is better for you to be persecuted than to be allowed to live too easily. The other day, I put some primroses in my conservatory; those that were left out in the open, to endure the cold windy nights, bloomed splendidly; but those that were in the warmer atmosphere did not get on nearly so well. There are some Christians that are like the primrose, they need a little cold weather, and do not get on so well where it is too warm. The Lord sends you opposition to make you all the stronger. But the bands of the wicked cannot hold you; break loose from them, I pray you, through the power God gives you by his grace.

"Ah!" you say, "but Satan himself breaks in upon me." Very likely he does; but just resist him, steadfast in the faith. Possibly he is throwing blasphemies into your mind, injecting evil thoughts which you never had before. But, if a thousand devils were to bind you thus with cords, so that you could not move hand or foot, yet, depend upon it, you shall slip out of the cords, and come into perfect liberty, for all the devils in hell cannot hold a soul that belongs to Christ, and you do belong to him if you truly trust him.

Perhaps I am also speaking to *some child of God who has fallen into great trouble*. You are an old Christian, and yet you have got into a bad scrape. You were never in such a condition before, and you seem to be bound with the cords of trouble after trouble, as if they were tightly knotted around you so that you could not get loose. There are also the cords of depression of spirit, and they sometimes cut very painfully, and hold you bound like a poor captive. Perhaps also the devil, as well as your own depression, has tied you up. There is a diabolical temptation that has come to you; you are even afraid that you are not a child of God at all, and you begin to doubt everything. You were never before bound as you are now; you seem to be thrust into the inner prison, and your feet made fast in the stocks. If so, I believe that God has sent me to do to you as the angel did to Peter. You know that the angel went to Peter, when he was asleep in the prison, and smote him on the side. Well, I cannot get near enough to you to do that, so you must take it as done. Then what did the angel do to Peter? He raised him up, his chains fell off from his hands, and the angel said to him, "Gird thyself, and bind on thy sandals. And so he did." Then the angel said, "Cast thy garment about thee, and follow me"; and Peter did so, and he walked through the first and the second ward of the prison. At last, they came to the iron gate leading into the city, that great gate that needed half-a-dozen men to open it, and Peter was surprised to see it open of its own accord. He never saw anything like that before, and soon he found himself with the cool night air playing on his forehead, and he was a free man again. All the Herods and all the devils cannot shut up a man who trusts in God; so, you will come out of your prison again. You are like a cork in the water; men may press you below the surface, but you are bound to come to the top again. You know what Haman planned for Mordecai; he meant to hang him up on the high gallows that he had erected. He was not satisfied with that, for he intended also to kill all who belonged to the same race as Mordecai; he meant that not a Jew should be allowed to live; but, when his plans could not be carried out as he intended, his wise men and his wife said to him, "If Mordecai be of the seed of the Jews, before whom thou hast begun to fall, thou shalt not prevail against him, but shalt surely fall before him"; and so it came to pass, for there swung Haman on the gallows that he had erected for the execution of Mordecai. There may be a Haman plotting against you; leave him alone. If he is making the gallows, let him finish them; they will come in for himself in due time. If you belong to Jesus Christ, and if you belong to the seed of the believers, before whom Satan had begun to fall, he will never prevail against you, but you will overcome him, for you must reign with Christ for ever, for he himself has said so.

Finally, beloved, there is a part of Christ's redeemed possession that is under mortgage at present; it is not yet delivered from the bond that holds it. What part is that? It is *this poor body, these bones, and this flesh and blood*, for although "the spirit is life because of righteousness," the body is still "dead because of sin." And soon, that poor body of yours, unless Christ shall come first, will see corruption, and moulder, and go back to dust; but mark this, as I have already said, Christ will not leave any fragment of his people in the hands of the enemy; he will not leave any portion of his people—no, not so much as a bone of them,—under the dominion of death. The hour shall come when the trumpet shall sound, and the dead shall be raised; and, as the soul has been redeemed, so shall the body also enter into the fullness of the joy of adoption, to wit, the redemption of the body. We have buried many of the godly; there is many a *Campo Santo* ("Holy Ground") round about this great city, where sleep the pious dead; and we have wept as we have committed them to the silent clay. But they are not lost,—not one of them is lost. No baby, chosen of God to see heaven ere it saw much of the world, no man or woman in middle life, taken from the midst of the conflict, no grey-headed man, who leaned upon his staff for very age and came to the grave like a shock of corn to the garner; there shall not one of them be lost, nor an eye, nor a foot, nor a hand of any one of them; yea, and the very hairs of their head are all numbered. The Lord hath taken an inventory of all that he has bought with his precious blood, and he will have it all; not merely the souls and spirits of his people, but their bodies, too. Who is to stop him? Death knows his power, but must yield to it. The strong man armed did keep the sepulchre, but a stronger than he came in, and burst the bands of the tomb, and he came forth alive; and—

> *As the Lord our Saviour rose,*
> *So all his followers must;*

for, as it is written, "A bone of him shall not be broken"; and it is not possible that they, who are, as it were, the bones of his mystical body, should be holden by the bonds of death. O happy people, who belong to Christ! God grant that we may all be numbered amongst them, for his great name's sake!

4

THE ASCENSION PRACTICALLY CONSIDERED

"And while they looked steadfastly toward heaven as he
went up, behold, two men stood by them in white apparel;
which also said, Ye men of Galilee, why stand ye gazing up
into heaven? this same Jesus, which is taken up from you into
heaven, shall so come in like manner as ye have seen him go
into heaven."—Acts 1: 10, 11.

FOUR great events shine out brightly in our Saviour's story.
All Christian minds delight to dwell upon his birth, his death,
his resurrection, and his ascension. These make four rounds in
that ladder of light, the foot of which is upon the earth, but the
top whereof reacheth to heaven. We could not afford to dis-
pense with any one of those four events, nor would it be profit-
able for us to forget, or to under-estimate, the value of any one
of them. That the Son of God was born of a woman creates in
us the intense delight of a brotherhood springing out of a
common humanity. That Jesus once suffered unto the death for
our sins, and thereby made a full atonement for us, is the rest
and life of our spirits. The manger and the cross together are
divine seals of love. That the Lord Jesus rose again from the
dead is the warrant of our justification, and also a transcen-
dently delightful assurance of the resurrection of all his people,
and of their eternal life in him. Hath he not said, "Because I
live, ye shall live also"? The resurrection of Christ is the
morning star of our future glory. Equally delightful is the
remembrance of his ascension. No song is sweeter than this—
"Thou hast ascended on high; thou hast led captivity
captive, thou hast received gifts for men, yea, for the rebellious also, that the Lord God might dwell among them"
(Ps. 68: 18).

Each one of those four events points to another, and they all
lead up to it: the fifth link in the golden chain is our Lord's

second and most glorious advent. Nothing is mentioned
between his ascent and his descent. True, a rich history comes
between; but it lies in a valley between two stupendous mountains: we step from alp to alp as we journey in meditation
from the ascension to the second advent. I say that each of
the previous four events points to it. Had he not come a first
time in humiliation, born under the law, he could not have come
a second time in amazing glory "without a sin-offering unto
salvation." Because he died once, we rejoice that he dieth no
more, death hath no more dominion over him, and therefore
he cometh to destroy that last enemy whom he hath already
conquered. It is our joy, as we think of our Redeemer as risen,
to feel that, in consequence of his rising, the trump of the archangel shall assuredly sound for the awaking of all his slumbering
people, when the Lord himself shall descend from heaven with
a shout. As for his ascension, he could not a second time
descend if he had not first ascended; but having perfumed
heaven with his presence, and prepared a place for his people,
we may fitly expect that he will come again and receive us
unto himself, that where he is there we may be also. I want you,
therefore, as in contemplation you pass with joyful footsteps
over these four grand events, as your faith leaps from his birth
to his death, and from his resurrection to his ascension, to be
looking forward, and even hastening, unto this crowning fact
of our Lord's history; for ere long he shall so come in like
manner as he was seen go up into heaven.

To-day, in our meditation, we will start from the ascension;
and if I had sufficient imagination I should like to picture our
Lord and the eleven walking up the side of Olivet, communing
as they went, a happy company, with a solemn awe upon them,
but with an intense joy in having fellowship with each other.
Each disciple was glad to think that his dear Lord and Master
who had been crucified was now among them, not only alive
but surrounded with a mysterious safety and glory which none
could disturb. The enemy was as still as a stone: not a dog
moved his tongue: his bitterest foes made no sign during the
days of our Lord's after-life below. The company moved
onward peacefully towards Bethany—Bethany which they all
knew and loved. The Saviour seemed drawn there at the time
of his ascension, even as men's minds return to old and well-

loved scenes when they are about to depart out of this world. His happiest moments on earth had been spent beneath the roof where lived Mary and Martha and their brother Lazarus. Perhaps it was best for the disciples that he should leave them at that place where he had been most hospitably entertained, to show that he departed in peace and not in anger. There they had seen Lazarus raised from the dead by him who was now to be taken up from them: the memory of the triumphant past would help the tried faith of the present. There they had heard the voice saying, "Loose him, and let him go," and there they might fitly see their Lord loosed from all bonds of earthly gravitation that he might go to his Father and their Father. The memories of the place might help to calm their minds and arouse their spirits to that fulness of joy which ought to attend the glorifying of their Lord.

But they have come to a standstill, having reached the brow of the hill. The Saviour stands conspicuously in the centre of the group, and, following upon most instructive discourse, he pronounces a blessing upon them. He lifts his pierced hands, and, while he is lifting them and is pronouncing words of love, he begins to rise from the earth. He has risen above them all to their astonishment! In a moment he has passed beyond the olives, which seem with their silvery sheen to be lit up by his milder radiance. While the disciples are looking, the Lord has ascended into mid air, and speedily he has risen to the regions of the clouds. They stand spell-bound with astonishment, and suddenly a bright cloud, like a chariot of God, bears him away. That cloud conceals him from mortal gaze. Though we have known Christ after the flesh, now after the flesh know we him no more. They are riveted to the spot, very naturally so: they linger long in the place; they stand with streaming eyes, wonder-struck, still looking upward.

It is not the Lord's will that they should long remain inactive; their reverie is interrupted. They might have stood there till wonder saddened into fear. As it was, they remained long enough; for the angel's words may be accurately rendered, "Why have ye stood, gazing up into heaven?"

Their lengthened gaze needed to be interrupted, and, therefore, two shining ones, such as aforetime met the women at the sepulchre, are sent to them. These messengers of God appear in human form that they may not alarm them, and in white raiment as if to remind them that all was bright and joyous; and these white-robed ministers stood with them as if they would willingly join their company. As no one of the eleven would break silence, the men in white raiment commenced the discourse. Addressing them in the usual celestial style, they asked a question which contained its own answer, and then went on to tell their message. As they had once said to the women, "Why seek ye the living among the dead? He is not here, but is risen;" so did they now say, "Ye men of Galilee, why stand ye gazing up into heaven? this same Jesus, which is taken up from you into heaven, shall so come in like manner as ye have seen him go into heaven." The angels showed their knowledge of them by calling them "men of Galilee," and reminded them that they were yet upon earth by recalling their place of birth.

Brought back to their senses, their reverie over, the apostles at once gird up their loins for active service; they do not need twice telling, but hasten to Jerusalem. The vision of angels has singularly enough brought them back into the world of actual life again, and they obey the command, "Tarry ye at Jerusalem." They seem to say, The taking up of our Master is not a thing to weep about: he has gone to his throne and to his glory, and he said it was expedient for us that he should go away. He will now send us the promise of the Father; we scarcely know what it will be like, but let us, in obedience to his will, make the best of our way to the place where he bade us await the gift of power. Do you not see them going down the side of Olivet, taking that Sabbath-day's journey into the cruel and wicked city without a thought of fear: having no dread of the bloodthirsty crew who slew their Lord, but happy in the memory of their Lord's exaltation and in the expectation of a wonderful display of his power. They held fellowship of the most delightful kind with one another, and anon entered into the upper room, where, in protracted prayer and communion, they waited for the promise of the Father. You see I have no imagination: I have barely mentioned the incidents in the simplest language. Yet try and realise the scene, for it will be helpful so to do, since our Lord Jesus is to come in like manner as the disciples saw him go up into heaven.

My first business will be to consider *the gentle chiding* administered by the shining ones:—"Ye men of Galilee, why stand ye gazing up into heaven?" Secondly, *the cheering description* of our Lord which the white-robed messengers used,—"This same Jesus"; and then, thirdly, *the practical truth* which they taught —"This same Jesus, which is taken up from you into heaven, shall so come in like manner as ye have seen him go into heaven."

First, then, here is A GENTLE CHIDING. It is not sharply uttered by men dressed in black who use harsh speech, and upbraid the servants of God severely for what was rather a mistake than a fault. No; the language is strengthening, yet tender: the fashion of a question allows them rather to reprove themselves than to be reproved; and the tone is that of brotherly love, and affectionate concern.

Notice, that *what these saintly men were doing seems at first sight to be very right.* Methinks, if Jesus were among us now we would fix our eyes upon him, and never withdraw them. He is altogether lovely, and it would seem wicked to yield our eyesight to any inferior object so long as he was to be seen. When he ascended up into heaven it was the duty of his friends to look upon him. It can never be wrong to look up; we are often bidden to do so, and it is even a holy saying of the Psalmist, "I will direct my prayer unto thee, and will look up"; and, again, "I will lift up mine eyes unto the hills, from whence cometh my help." If it be right to look up into heaven, it must be still more right to look up while Jesus rises to the place of his glory. Surely it had been wrong if they had looked anywhere else,—it was due to the Lamb of God that they should behold him as long as eyes could follow him. He is the Sun: where should eyes be turned but to his light? He is the King; and where should courtiers within the palace gate turn their eyes but to their King as he ascends to his throne?

The truth is, there was nothing wrong in their looking up into heaven; but they went a little further than looking; they stood "gazing." A little excess in right may be faulty. It may be wise to look, but foolish to gaze. There is a very thin partition sometimes between that which is commendable and that which is censurable. There is a golden mean which it is not easy to keep. The exact path of right is often as narrow as a razor's edge, and he must be wise that doth not err either on the right hand or on the left. "Look" is ever the right word. Why, it is "Look unto me, and be saved." Look, aye, look steadfastly and intently: be your posture that of one "looking unto Jesus," always throughout life. But there is a gazing which is not commendable, when the look becomes not that of reverent worship, but of an overweening curiosity; when there mingles with the desire to know what should be known, a prying into that which it is for God's glory to conceal. It is of little use to look up into an empty heaven.

If Christ himself be not visible in heaven, then in vain do we gaze, since there is nothing for a saintly eye to see. When the Person of Jesus was gone out of the azure vault above them and the cloud had effectually concealed him, why should they continue to gaze when God himself had drawn the curtain? If infinite wisdom had withdrawn the object upon which they desired to gaze, what would their gazing be but a sort of reflection upon the wisdom which had removed their Lord? Yet it did seem very right. Thus certain things that you and I may do may appear right, and yet we may need to be chidden out of them into something better: they may be right in themselves but not appropriate for the occasion, not seasonable, nor expedient. They may be right up to a point, and then may touch the boundary of excess. A steadfast gaze into heaven may be to a devout soul a high order of worship, but if this filled up much of our working time it might become the idlest form of folly.

Yet I cannot help adding that *it was very natural*. I do not wonder that the whole eleven stood gazing up, for if I had been there I am sure I should have done the same. How struck they must have been with the ascent of the Master out of their midst! You would be amazed if some one from among our own number now began to ascend into heaven, would you not? Our Lord did not gradually melt away from sight as a phantom, or dissolve into thin air as a mere apparition: the Saviour did not disappear in that way at all, but he rose, and they saw that it was his very self that was so rising. His own body, the materialism in which he had veiled himself, actually, distinctly and literally, rose to heaven before their eyes. I repeat, the Lord did not dissolve, and disappear like a vision of the night,

46

but he evidently rose till the cloud intervened so that they could see him no more. I think I should have stood looking to the very place where his cloudy chariot had been. I know it would be idle to continue so to do, but our hearts often urge us on to acts which we could not justify logically. Hearts are not to be argued with.

Sometimes you stand by a grave where one is buried whom you dearly loved: you go there often to weep. You cannot help it, the place is precious to you; yet you could not prove that you do any good by your visits, perhaps you even injure yourself thereby, and deserve to be gently chidden with the question, "Why?" It may be the most natural thing in the world, and yet it may not be a wise thing. The Lord allows us to do that which is innocently natural, but he will not have us carry it too far; for then it might foster an evil nature. Hence he sends an interrupting messenger: not an angel with a sword, or even a rod; but he sends some man in white raiment,—I mean one who is both cheerful and holy, and he, by his conduct or his words, suggests to us the question, "Why stand ye here gazing?" *Cui bono?* What will be the benefit? What will it avail? Thus our understanding being called into action, and we being men of thought, we answer to ourselves, "This will not do. We must not stand gazing here for ever," and therefore we arouse ourselves to get back to the Jerusalem of practical life, where in the power of God we hope to do service for our Master.

Notice, then, that the disciples were doing that which seemed to be right, and what was evidently very natural, but that it is very easy to carry the apparently right and the absolutely natural too far. Let us take heed to ourselves, and often ask our hearts, "Why?"

For, thirdly, notice that what they *did was not after all justifiable upon strict reason.* While Christ was going up it was proper that they should adoringly look at him. He might almost have said, "If ye see me when I am taken up a double portion of my spirit shall rest upon you." They did well to look where he led the way. But, when he was gone, still to remain gazing was an act which they could not exactly explain to themselves, and could not justify to others. Put the question thus: "What purpose will be fulfilled by your continuing to

47

gaze into the sky? He is gone; it is absolutely certain that he is gone. He is taken up, and God himself has manifestly concealed all trace of him by bidding yonder cloud sail in between him and you. Why gaze ye still? He told you 'I go unto my Father.' Why stand and gaze?" We may, under the influence of great love, act unwisely. I remember well seeing the action of a woman whose only son was emigrating to a distant colony. I stood in the station, and I noticed her many tears and her frequent embraces of her boy; but the train came up, and he entered the carriage. After the train had passed beyond the station, she was foolish enough to break away from friends who sought to detain her; she ran along the platform, leaped down upon the railroad and pursued the flying train. It was natural, but it had been better left undone. What was the use of it? We had better abstain from acts which serve no practical purpose; for in this life we have neither time nor strength to waste in fruitless action. The disciples would be wise to cease gazing, for nobody would be benefited by it, and they would not themselves be blessed. What is the use of gazing when there is nothing to see? Well, then, did the angels ask, "Why stand ye gazing up into heaven?"

Again, put another question: What precept were they obeying when they stood gazing up into heaven? If you have a command from God to do a certain thing, you need not inquire into the reason of the command, it is disobedient to begin to canvas God's will; but when there is no precept whatever, why persevere in an act which evidently does not promise to bring any blessing? Who bade them stand gazing up into heaven? If Christ had done so, then in Christ's name let them stand like statues and never turn their heads: but, as he had not bidden them, why did they do what he had not commanded, and leave undone what he had commanded? For he had strictly charged them that they should tarry at Jerusalem till they were "endued with power from on high." So what they did was not justifiable.

Here is the practical point for us: *What they did we are very apt to imitate.* "Oh," say you, "I shall never stand gazing up into heaven." I am not sure of that. Some Christians are very curious, but not obedient. Plain precepts are neglected, but difficult problems they seek to solve. I remember one who used always to be dwelling upon the vials and seals and trumpets. He was great at apocalyptic symbols; but he had seven children, and he had no family prayer. If he had left the vials and trumpets and minded his boys and girls, it would have been a deal better. I have known men marvellously great upon Daniel, and specially instructed in Ezekiel, but singularly forgetful of the twentieth of Exodus, and not very clear upon Romans the eighth. I do not speak with any blame of such folks for studying Daniel and Ezekiel, but quite the reverse; yet I wish they had been more zealous for the conversion of the sinners in their neighbourhoods, and more careful to assist the poor saints. I admit the value of the study of the feet of the image in Nebuchadnezzar's vision, and the importance of knowing the kingdoms which make up the ten toes, but I do not see the propriety of allowing such studies to overlay the common-places of practical godliness. If the time spent over obscure theological propositions were given to a mission in the dim alley near the good man's house, more benefit would come to men and more glory to God. I would have you understand all mysteries, if you could; but do not forget that our chief business here below is to cry, "Behold the Lamb!" By all manner of means read and search till you know all that the Lord has revealed concerning things to come; but, first of all, see to it that your children are brought to the Saviour's feet, and that you are workers together with God in the upbuilding of his church. The dense mass of misery and ignorance and sin which is round about us on every side demands all our powers; and, if you do not respond to the call, though I am not a man in white apparel, I shall venture to say to you, "Ye men of Christendom, why stand ye gazing up into the mysteries when so much is to be done for Jesus, and you are leaving it undone?" O ye who are curious but not obedient, I fear I speak to you in vain, but I have spoken. May the Holy Spirit also speak.

Others are contemplative but not active,—much given to the study of Scripture and to meditation thereon, but not zealous for good works. Contemplation is so scarce in these days that I could wish there were a thousand times as much of it; but, in the case to which I refer, everything runs in the one channel of thought, all time is spent in reading, in enjoyment, in rapture, in pious leisure. Religion never ought to become the subject of selfishness, and yet I fear some treat it as if its chief end was spiritual gratification. When a man's religion all lies in his saving his own self, and in enjoying holy things for his own self, there is a disease upon him. When his judgment of a sermon is based upon the one question, "Did it feed *me*?" it is a swinish judgment. There is such a thing as getting a swinish religion in which you are yourself first, yourself second, yourself third, yourself to the utmost end. Did Jesus ever think or speak in that fashion? Contemplation of Christ himself may be so carried out as to lead you away from Christ : the recluse meditates on Jesus, but he is as unlike the busy self-denying Jesus as well can be. Meditation unattended with active service in the spreading of the gospel among men, well deserves the rebuke of the angel, "Ye men of Galilee, why stand ye gazing up into heaven?"

Moreover, some are careful and anxious and deliriously impatient for some marvellous interposition. We get at times into a sad state of mind, because we do not see the kingdom of Christ advancing as we desire. I suppose it is with you as it is with me. I begin to fret, and I am deeply troubled, and I feel that there is good reason that I should be, for truth is fallen in the streets, and the days of blasphemy and rebuke are upon us. Then we pine ; for the Master is away, and we cry, "When will he be back again? Oh, why are his chariots so long in coming? Why tarries he through the ages?" Our desires sour into impatience, and we commence gazing up into heaven, looking for his coming with a restlessness which does not allow us to discharge our duty as we should. Whenever anybody gets into that state, this is the word, "Ye men of Galilee, why stand ye gazing up into heaven?"

In certain cases this uneasiness has drawn to itself a wrong expectation of immediate wonders, and an intense desire for sign-seeing. Ah me, what fanaticisms come of this! In America years ago, one came forward who declared that on such a day the Lord would come, and he led a great company to believe his crazy predictions. Many took their horses and fodder for two or three days, and went out into the woods, expecting to be all the more likely to see all that was to be seen when once away from the crowded city. All over the States there were people who had made ascension-dresses in which to soar into the air in proper costume. They waited, and they waited, and

I am sure that no text could have been more appropriate for them than this, "Ye men of America, why stand ye here gazing up into heaven?" Nothing came of it; and yet there are thousands in England and America who only need a fanatical leader, and they would run into the like folly. The desire to know the times and seasons is a craze with many poor bodies whose insanity runs in that particular groove. Every occurrence is a "sign of the times": a sign, I may add, which they do not understand. An earthquake is a special favourite with them. "Now," they cry, "the Lord is coming"; as if there had not been earthquakes of the sort we have heard of lately hundreds of times since our Lord went up into heaven. When the prophetic earthquakes occur in divers places, we shall know of it without the warnings of these brethren. What a number of persons have been infatuated by the number of the beast, and have been ready to leap for joy because they have found the number 666 in some great one's name. Why, everybody's name will yield that number if you treat it judiciously, and use the numerals of Greece, Rome, Egypt, China, or Timbuctoo. I feel weary with the silly way in which some people make toys out of Scripture, and play with texts as with a pack of cards. Whenever you meet with a man who sets up to be a prophet, keep out of his way in the future; and when you hear of signs and wonders, turn you to your Lord, and in patience possess your souls. "The just shall live by his faith." There is no other way of living among wild enthusiasts. Believe in God, and ask not for miracles and marvels, or the knowledge of times and seasons. To know when the Lord will restore the kingdom is not in your power. Remember that verse: "It is not for you to know the times or the seasons." If I were introduced into a room where a large number of parcels were stored up, and I were told that there was something good for me, I should begin to look for that which had my name upon it, and when I came upon a parcel, and I saw, in pretty big letters, "*It is not for you*," I should leave it alone. Here, then, is a casket of knowledge marked, "*It is not for you* to know the times or the seasons, which the Father hath put in his own power." Cease to meddle with matters which are concealed, and be satisfied to know the things which are clearly revealed.

Secondly, I want you to notice THE CHEERING DESCRIPTION

which these bright spirits give concerning our Lord. They describe him thus,—"This same Jesus."

I appreciate the description the more because *it came from those who knew him.* "He was seen of angels"; they had watched him all his life long, and they knew him, and, when they, having just seen him rise to his Father and his God, said of him, "This same Jesus," then I know by an infallible testimony that he was the same, and that he is the same.

Jesus is gone, but he still exists. He has left us, but he is not dead; he has not dissolved into nothing like the mist of the morning. "This same Jesus" is gone up unto his Father's throne, and he is there to-day as certainly as he once stood at Pilate's bar. As surely as he did hang upon the cross, so surely does he, the self-made man, sit upon the throne of God and reign over creation. I like to think of the positive identity of the Christ in the seventh heaven with the Christ in the lowest deeps of agony. The Christ they spat upon is now the Christ whose name the cherubim and seraphim are hymning day without night. The Christ they scourged is he before whom principalities and powers delight to cast their crowns. Think of it and be glad; and do not stand gazing up into heaven after a myth or a dream. Jesus lives; mind that you live also. Do not loiter as if you had nothing at all to do, or as if the kingdom of God had come to an end because Jesus is gone from the earth, as to his bodily Presence. It is not all over; he still lives, and he has given you a work to do till he comes. Therefore, go and do it.

"This same Jesus"—I love that word, for "Jesus" means *a Saviour.* Oh, ye anxious sinners here present, the name of him who has gone up into his glory is full of invitation to you! Will you not come to "this same Jesus"? This is he who opened the eyes of the blind and brought forth the prisoners out of the prison-house. He is doing the same thing to-day. Oh that your eyes may see his light! He that touched the lepers, and that raised the dead, is the same Jesus still, able to save to the uttermost. Oh that you may look and live! You have only to come to him by faith, as she did who touched the hem of his garment; you have but to cry to him as the blind man did whose sight he restored; for he is the same Jesus, bearing about with him the same tender love for guilty men, and the same readiness to receive and cleanse all that come to him by faith.

"This same Jesus." Why, that must have meant that he who is in heaven is the same Christ who was on earth, but it must also mean that *he who is to come will be the same Jesus that went up into heaven.* There is no change in our blessed Master's nature, nor will there ever be. There is a great change in his condition:—

> *The Lord shall come, but not the same*
> *As once in lowliness he came,*
> *A humble man before his foes,*
> *A weary man, and full of woes.*

He will be "the same Jesus" in nature though not in condition: he will possess the same tenderness when he comes to judge, the same gentleness of heart when all the glories of heaven and earth shall gird his brow. Our eye shall see him in that day, and we shall recognize him not only by the nail-prints, but by the very look of his countenance, by the character that gleams from that marvellous face; and we shall say, "'Tis he! 'tis he! the self-same Christ that went up from the top of Olivet from the midst of his disciples." Go to him with your troubles, as you would have done when he was here. Look forward to his second coming without dread. Look for him with that joyous expectancy with which you would welcome Jesus of Bethany, who loved Mary, and Martha, and Lazarus.

On the back of that sweet title came this question, "Why stand ye here gazing into heaven?" They might have said, "We stay here because we do not know where to go. Our Master is gone." But it is the same Jesus, and he is coming again, so go down to Jerusalem and get to work directly. Do not worry yourselves; no grave accident has occurred; it is not a disaster that Christ has gone, but an advance in his work. Despisers tell us nowadays, "Your cause is done for! Christianity is spun out! Your divine Christ is gone; we have not seen a trace of his miracle-working hand, nor of that voice which no man could rival." Here is our answer: We are not standing gazing up into heaven, we are not paralysed because Jesus is away. He lives, the great Redeemer lives; and, though it is our delight to lift up our eyes because we expect his coming, it is equally our delight to turn our heavenly gazing into an earthward watching, and to go down into the city, and there to tell that Jesus is risen, that men are to be saved by faith in him, and that whosoever believeth in him shall have everlasting life. We are not defeated, far from it: his ascension is not a retreat, but an advance. His tarrying is not for want of power, but because of the abundance of his long-suffering. The victory is not questionable. All things work for it; all the hosts of God are mustering for the final charge. "This same Jesus" is mounting his white horse to lead forth the armies of heaven, conquering and to conquer.

Our third point is this, THE GREAT PRACTICAL TRUTH. This truth is not one that is to keep us gazing into heaven, but one that is to make each of us go to his house to render earnest service. What is it?

Why, first, that *Jesus is gone into heaven*. Jesus is gone! Jesus is gone! It sounds like a knell. Jesus is taken up from you into heaven! That sounds like a marriage peal. He is gone, but he is gone up to the hills whence he can survey the battle; up to the throne, from which he can send us succour. The reserve forces of the omnipotent stood waiting till their Captain came, and now that he is come into the centre of the universe, he can send legions of angels, or he can raise up hosts of men for the help of his cause. I see every reason for going down into the world and getting to work, for he is gone up into heaven and "all power is given unto him in heaven and in earth." Is not that a good argument, "Go ye *therefore* and teach all nations, baptising them in the name of the Father, and of the Son, and of the Holy Ghost"?

Jesus will come again. That is another reason for girding our loins, because it is clear that he has not quitted the fight, nor deserted the field of battle. Our great Captain is still heading the conflict; he has ridden into another part of the field, but he will be back again, perhaps in the twinkling of an eye. You do not say that a commander has given up the campaign because it is expedient that he should withdraw from your part of the field. Our Lord is doing the best thing for his kingdom in going away. It was in the highest degree expedient that he should go, and that we should each one receive the Spirit. There is a blessed unity between Christ the King and the commonest soldier in the ranks. He has not taken his heart from us, nor his care from us, nor his interest from us: he is bound up heart and soul with his people and their holy warfare, and this is the evidence of it, "Behold, I come quickly; and my reward is with me, to give every man according as his work shall be" (Rev. 22:12).

Then, moreover, we are told in the text—and this is a reason why we should get to our work—that *he is coming in like manner as he departed*. Certain of the commentators do not seem to understand English at all. "He which is taken up from you into heaven shall so come in like manner as you have seen him go into heaven"; this, they say, relates to his spiritual coming at Pentecost. Give anybody a grain of sense, and do they not see that a spiritual coming is not a coming in the same manner in which he went up into heaven? There is an analogy, but certainly not a likeness between the two things. Our Lord was taken up; they could see him rise: he will come again, and "every eye shall see him." He went up not in Spirit, but in Person: he will come down in person. "This same Jesus shall so come in like manner." He went up, not in poetic figure and spiritual symbol, but as a matter of fact. "This same Jesus" literally went up. "This same Jesus" will literally come again. He will descend in clouds even as he went up in clouds; and "he shall stand at the latter day upon the earth," even as he stood aforetime. He went up to heaven unopposed; no high priests, nor scribes, nor Pharisees, nor even one of the rabble opposed his ascension; it were ridiculous to suppose that they could; and when he comes a second time none will stand against him. His adversaries shall perish; as the fat of rams shall they melt away in his Presence. When he cometh he shall break rebellious nations with a rod of iron, for his force shall be irresistible in that day.

Do not let anybody spiritualize away all this from you. Jesus is coming as a matter of fact, therefore go down to your sphere of service as a matter of fact. Get to work and teach the ignorant, win the wayward, instruct the children, and everywhere tell out the sweet name of Jesus. As a matter of fact, give of your substance and don't talk about it. As a matter of fact, consecrate your daily life to the glory of God. As a matter of fact, live wholly for your Redeemer. Jesus is not coming in a sort of mythical, misty, hazy way, he is literally and actually coming, and he will literally and actually call upon you to give an account of your stewardship.

For this is what the men in white apparel meant, *be ready to meet your coming Lord*. What is the way to be ready to meet Jesus? If it is the same Jesus that went away from us who is coming, then let us be doing what he was doing before he went away. If it is the same Jesus that is coming we cannot possibly put ourselves into a posture of which he will better approve than by going about doing good. If you would meet him with joy, serve him with earnestness. If the Lord Jesus Christ were to come to-day I should like him to find me at my studying, praying, or preaching. Would you not like him to find you in your Sunday-school, in your class, or out there at the corner of the street preaching, or doing whatever you have the privilege of doing in his name? Would you meet your Lord in idleness? Do not think of it. I called one day on one of our members, and she was whitening the front steps. She got up all in confusion; she said, "Oh dear, sir, I did not know you were coming to-day, or I would have been ready." I replied, "Dear friend, you could not be in better trim than you are: you are doing your duty like a good housewife, and may God bless you." She had no money to spare for a servant, and she was doing her duty by keeping the home tidy: I thought she looked more beautiful with her pail beside her than if she had been dressed according to the latest fashion. I said to her, "When the Lord Jesus Christ comes suddenly, I hope he will find me doing as you were doing, namely, fulfilling the duty of the hour." I want you all to get to your pails without being ashamed of them. Serve the Lord in some way or other; serve him always; serve him intensely; serve him more and more. Go to-morrow and serve the Lord at the counter, or in the workshop, or in the field. Go and serve the Lord by helping the poor and the needy, the widow and the fatherless; serve him by teaching the children, especially by endeavouring to train your own children. Go and hold a temperance meeting, and show the drunkard that there is hope for him in Christ, or go to the midnight meeting and let the fallen woman know that Jesus can restore her. Do what Jesus has given you the power to do, and then, when he comes he will say to you, "Well done, good and faithful servant, enter thou into the joy of thy Lord." So may his grace enable us to do.

5

THE HOLY SPIRIT GLORIFYING CHRIST

"He shall glorify me: for he shall receive of mine, and shall shew it unto you."—John 16: 14.

THE needs of spiritual men are very great, but they cannot be greater than the power of the Divine Trinity is able to meet. We have one God,—Father, Son, and Holy Ghost,—One in Three, and Three in One; and that blessed Trinity in Unity gives himself to sinners that they may be saved. In the first place, every good thing that a sinner wants is in the Father. The prodigal son was wise when he said, "I will arise and go to my father." Every good and perfect gift comes from God the Father, the first Person in the blessed Trinity, because every good gift and every perfect gift can only be found in him. But the needy soul says, "How shall I get to the Father? He is infinitely above me. How shall I reach up to him?" In order that you might obtain the blessings of grace, God was in Christ Jesus, the second ever-blessed Person of the Sacred Trinity. Let me read you part of the verse that follows my text: "All things that the Father hath are mine." So, you see, everything is in the Father first; and the Father puts all things into Christ. "It pleased the Father that in him should all fulness dwell" (Col. 1: 19). Now you can get to Christ because he is man as well as God. He is "over all, God blessed for ever;" but he came into this world, was born of the Virgin Mary, lived a life of poverty, "suffered under Pontius Pilate, was crucified, dead, and buried." He is the conduit-pipe, conveying to us all blessings from the Father. In the Gospel of John we read, "Of his fulness have all we received, and grace for grace." Thus you see the Father, with every good thing in himself, putting all fulness into the Mediator, the Man Christ Jesus who is also the Son of God.

Now I hear a poor soul say, "But I cannot even get to Christ; I am blind and lame. If I could get to him, he would open my eyes; but I am so lame that I cannot run or even walk to him. If I could get to him, he would give me strength; but I lie as one dead. I cannot see Christ, or tell where to find him." Here comes in the work of the Holy Spirit, the third Person of the blessed Unity. It is his office to take of the things of Christ, and show them unto saints and sinners, too. We cannot see them, but we shall see them fast enough when he shows them to us. Our sin puts a veil between us and Christ. The Holy Spirit comes and takes the veil away from our heart, and then we see Christ. It is the Holy Spirit's office to come between us and Christ, to lead us to Christ, even as the Son of God comes between us and the Father, to lead us to the Father; so that we have the whole Trinity uniting to save a sinner, the Triune God bowing down out of heaven for the salvation of rebellious men. Every time we dismiss you from this house of prayer, we pronounce upon you the blessing of the Sacred Trinity: "May the grace of our Lord Jesus Christ, and the love of God, and the communion of the Holy Ghost be with you!" And you want all that to make a sinner into a saint, and to keep a saint from going back to be a sinner again. The whole blessed Godhead, Father, Son, and Holy Spirit, must work upon every soul that is to be saved.

See how divinely they work together, how the Father glorifies the Son, how the Holy Spirit glorifies Jesus, how both the Holy Spirit and the Lord Jesus glorify the Father! These Three are One, sweetly uniting in the salvation of the chosen seed.

Now our work is to speak of the Holy Spirit. Oh, what a blessed Person he is; not merely a sacred influence, but a Divine Person, "very God of very God." He is the Spirit of holiness to be reverenced, to be spoken of with delight, yet with trembling; for, remember, there is a sin against the Holy Ghost. A word spoken against the Son of man may be forgiven, but blasphemy against the Holy Ghost (whatever that may be, I know not), is put down as a sin beyond the line of divine forgiveness. Therefore reverence, honour, and worship God the Holy Spirit, in whom lies the only hope that any of us can ever have of seeing Jesus, and so of seeing God the Father.

First, I shall try to speak of *what the Holy Spirit does:* "He shall receive of mine, and shall shew it unto you;" secondly, I shall seek to set forth *what the Holy Spirit aims at:* "He shall glorify me: for he shall receive of mine, and shall shew it unto you;" and, thirdly, I shall explain how *in both these things he acts as the Comforter*, for we read, in the seventh verse, that our Saviour says, "If I go not away, the Comforter will not come unto you;" and it is of the Comforter that he says, "He shall glorify me; for he shall receive of mine, and shall shew it unto you."

First, we are to consider WHAT THE HOLY SPIRIT DOES. Jesus says, "He shall receive of mine, and shall shew it unto you."

The Holy Ghost, then, *deals with the things of Christ*. How I wish that all Christ's ministers would imitate the Holy Spirit in this respect! When you are dealing with the things of Christ, you are on Holy Ghost ground; you are following the track of the Holy Spirit. Does the Holy Ghost deal with science? What is science? Another name for the ignorance of men. Does the Holy Ghost deal with politics? What are politics? Another name for every man getting as much as he can out of the nation. Does the Holy Ghost deal with these things? Nay, "He shall receive of mine." The Holy Ghost will leave you if you go gadding about after these insignificant trifles! He will leave you, if you aim at magnifying yourself, and your wisdom, and your plans; for the Holy Spirit is taken up with the things of Christ. "He shall receive of mine, and shall shew it unto you." I like what Mr. Wesley said to his preachers. "Leave other things alone," said he; "you are called to win souls." So I believe it is with all true preachers. We may let other things alone. The Holy Ghost, who is our Teacher, will own and bless us if we keep to his line of things. O preacher of the gospel, what canst thou receive like the things of Christ? And what canst thou talk of so precious to the souls of men as the things of Christ? Therefore, follow thou the Holy Ghost in dealing with the things of Christ.

Next, the Holy Spirit *deals with feeble men*. "He shall receive of mine, and shall shew it unto you." "Unto you." He is not above dealing with simple minds. He comes to those who have no training, no education, and he takes the things of Christ, and shows them to such minds. The greatest mind of man that was ever created was a poor puny thing compared with the infinite mind of God. We may boast about the great capacity of the human intellect; but what a narrow and contracted thing it is at its utmost width! So, for the Holy Spirit to come and teach the little mind of man, is a great condescension. But we see the great condescension of the Holy Ghost even more when we read, "Not many wise men after the flesh, not many mighty, not many noble, are called;" (1 Cor. 1: 26), and when we hear the Saviour say, "I thank thee, O Father, Lord of heaven and earth, because thou hast hid these things from the wise and prudent, and hast revealed them unto babes" (Matt. 11: 25). The Holy Ghost takes of the things of Christ, and shows them to those who are babes compared with the wise men of this world. The Lord Jesus might have selected princes to be his apostles; he might have gathered together twelve of the greatest kings of the earth, or at least twelve senators from Rome; but he did not so. He took fishermen, and men belonging to that class, to be the pioneers of his kingdom; and God the Holy Ghost takes of the things of Christ, high and sublime as they are, and shows them unto men like these apostles were, men ready to follow where the Lord led them, and to learn what the Lord taught them.

If you think of the condescension of the Holy Spirit in taking of the things of Christ, and showing them unto us, you will not talk any more about coming down to the level of children when you talk to them. I remember a young man, who was a great fool, but did not know it, and therefore was all the greater fool, once, speaking to children, said, "My dear children, it takes a great deal to bring a great mind down to your capacities." You cannot show me a word of Christ of that kind. Where does the Holy Ghost ever talk about its being a great come-down for him to teach children, or to teach us? Nay; but he glorifies Christ by taking of his things, and showing them unto us, even such poor ignorant scholars as we are.

If I understand what is meant here, I think that it means, first, that the Holy Ghost *helps us to understand the words of Christ*. If we will study the teaching of the Saviour, it must be with the Holy Spirit as the light to guide us; he will show us what Christ meant by the words he uttered. We shall not lose ourselves in the Saviour's verbiage; but we shall get at the inner meaning of Christ's mind, and be instructed therein; for the Lord Jesus says, "He shall receive of mine, and shall shew it unto you." A sermon of Christ, even a single word of Christ, set in the light of the Holy Spirit, shines like a diamond; nay, like a fixed star, with light that is never dim. Happy men and happy women who read the words of Christ in the light shed upon them by the Holy Ghost! But I do not think that this is all that the text means.

It means this: "Not only shall he reveal my words, but my *things;*" for Christ says, "All things that the Father hath are mine: therefore said I, that he shall take of mine, and shall shew it unto you."

The Holy Ghost takes the *nature* of Christ, and shows it unto us. It is easy to say, "I believe him to be God and man;" but the point is, to apprehend that he is God, and therefore able to save, and even to work impossibilities; and to believe that he is man, and therefore feels for you, sympathizes with you, and therefore is a brother born to help you in your adversities. May the Holy Ghost make you see the God-Man now. May he show you the humanity and the Deity of Christ, as they are most blessedly united in his adorable Person; and you will be greatly comforted thereby.

The Holy Ghost shows to us the *offices* of Christ. He is Prophet, Priest, King. Especially to you, sinner, Christ is a Saviour. Now, if you know that he takes up the work of saving sinners, and that it is his business to save men, why, then, surely you will have confidence in him, and not be afraid to come to him! If I wanted my shoes mended, I should not take my hat off when I went into a cobbler's shop, and say, "Please excuse me. May I beg you to be so good as to mend my shoes?" No, it is his trade: it is his business. He is glad to see me. "What do you want, sir?" says he; and he is glad of work. And when Christ puts over his door, "Saviour," I, wanting to be saved, go to him, for I believe that he knows his calling, and that he can carry it out, and that he will be glad to see me, and that I shall not be more glad to be saved than he will be to save me. I want you to catch that idea. If the Holy Spirit will show you that, it will bring you very near to joy and peace.

May the Holy Ghost also show you Christ's *engagements!* He has come into the world engaged to save sinners. He pledged himself to the Father to bring many sons unto glory, and he must do it. He has bound himself to his Father, as the Surety of the covenant, that he will bring sinners into reconciliation with

God. May the Holy Ghost show that fact to you; and right gladly you will leap into the Saviour's arms!

It is very sweet when the Holy Spirit shows us the *love* of Christ,—how intensely he loves men, how he loved them of old, for his delights were with the sons of men, not because he had redeemed them, but he redeemed them because he loved them, and delighted in them. Christ has had an eternal love to his people.

> *His heart is made of tenderness,*
> *His bowels melt with love.*

It is his heaven to bring men to heaven. It is his glory to bring sons to glory. He is never so happy as when he is receiving sinners. But if the Holy Ghost will show you the depth and the height, the length and the breadth, of the love of Christ to sinners, it will go a long way towards bringing all who are in this house to accept the Saviour.

But when the Holy Ghost shows you the *mercy* of Christ; how willingly he forgives; how he passes by iniquity, transgression, and sin; how he casts your sins into the sea, throws them behind God's back, puts them away for ever; ah! when you see this, then will your hearts be won to him.

Specially I would desire the Holy Ghost to show you the *blood* of Christ. A Spirit-taught view of the blood of Christ is the most wonderful sight that ever a weeping eye beheld. There is your sin, your wicked, horrible, damnable sin; but Christ comes into the world, and takes the sin, and suffers in your room and place and stead; and the blood of such an One as he, perfect Man and infinite God—such blood as was poured out on Calvary's tree,—must take away sin. Oh, for a sight of it! If any of you are now despairing, and the Holy Ghost will take of the blood of Christ, and show it unto you, despair will have no place in you any longer. It must be gone, for "the blood of Jesus Christ his Son cleanseth us from all sin," (1 John 1: 7), and he that believeth in him is forgiven all his iniquities.

And if the Holy Ghost will also take of the *prayers* of Christ, and show them unto you, what a sight you will have! Christ on earth, praying till he gets into a bloody sweat; Christ in heaven, praying with all his glorious vestments on, accepted by the Father, glorified at the Father's right hand, and making intercession for transgressors, praying for you, praying for all who come to God by him, and able, therefore, to save them to the uttermost; this is the sight you will have. A knowledge of the intercession of Christ for guilty men is enough to make despair flee away once for all. I can only tell you these things; but if the Holy Ghost will take of them, and show them unto you, oh, you will have joy and peace through believing!

One thing I must add, however, and then I will leave this point, upon which we could dilate for six months, I think; that is, that *whatever the Holy Ghost shows you, you may have.* Do you see that? He takes of the things of Christ, and shows them to us; but why? Not as a boy at school does to one of his companions when he is teasing him. I remember often seeing it done. He pulls out of his pocket a beautiful apple, and shows it to his schoolmate. "There," says he, "do you see that apple?" Is he going to say, "Now I am going to give you a piece of it"? No, not he. He only shows him the apple just to tantalize him. Now, it would be blasphemy to imagine that the Holy Ghost would show you the things of Christ, and then say, "You cannot have them." No, whatever he shows you, you may have. Whatever you see in Christ, you may have. Whatever the Holy Ghost makes you to see in the person and work of the Lord Jesus, you may have it. And he shows it to you on purpose that you may have it, for he is no Tantalus to mock us with the sight of a blessing beyond our reach; he waits to bless us. Lay that thought up in your heart; it may help you some day, if not now. You remember what God said to Jacob, "The land whereon thou liest, to thee will I give it"? If you find any promise in this Book, and you dare to lie down upon it, it is yours. If you can just lie down and rest on it, it is yours; for it was not put there for you to rest on it without its being fulfilled to you. Only stretch yourself on any covenant blessing, and it is yours for ever. God help us so to do!

But now, secondly, let us consider WHAT THE HOLY SPIRIT AIMS AT. Well, he aims at this, Jesus says, "He shall glorify me." When he shows us the things of Christ, his object is to glorify Christ. The Holy Spirit's object is to make Christ appear to be great and glorious to you and to me. The Lord Jesus Christ is infinitely glorious; and even the Holy Ghost cannot make him glorious except to our apprehension; but his desire is that we may see and know more of Christ, that we may honour him more, and glorify him more.

Well, how does the Holy Spirit go about this work? In this simple way, by *showing us the things of Christ*. Is not this a blessedly simple fact, that when even the Holy Ghost intends to glorify Christ, all that he does is to show us Christ? Well, but does he not put fine words together, and weave a spell of eloquence? No; he simply shows us Christ. Now, if you wanted to praise Jesus Christ, what would you have to do? Why, you would only have to speak of him as he is,—holy, blessed, glorious! You would show him, as it were, in order to praise him, for there is no glorifying Christ except by making him to be seen. Then he has the glory that rightly belongs to him. No words are wanted, no descriptions are needed. "He shall glorify me: for he shall receive of mine, and shall shew it unto you."

And is it not strange that Christ should be glorified by his *being shown to you? To you*. Perhaps you are saying, "I am a nobody." Yes, but Christ is glorified by being shown to you. "Oh, but I am very poor, very illiterate, and besides, very wicked!" Yes, but Christ is glorified by being shown to you. Now, a great king or a great queen would not be rendered much more illustrious by being shown to a little Sunday School girl, or exhibited to a crossing-sweeper boy. At least, they would not think so; but Christ does not act as an earthly monarch might. He reckons it to be his glory for the poorest pair of eyes that ever wept to look by faith upon him. He reckons it to be his greatest honour for the poorest man, the poorest woman, or the poorest child that ever lived, to see him in the light in which the Holy Ghost sets him. Is not this a blessed truth? I put it very simply and briefly. The Holy Ghost, you see, glorifies Christ by showing him to sinners. Therefore, if you want to glorify Christ, do the same. Do not go and write a ponderous tome, and put fine words together. Tell sinners, in simple language, what Christ is. "I cannot praise him," says one. You do not want to praise him. Say what he is. If a man says to me, "Show me the sun," do I say, "Well, you must wait till I strike a match and light a candle, and then I will show you the sun"? That would be ridiculous, would it not? And for our candles to be held up to show Christ, is absurd. Tell what he is. Tell what he is to you. Tell what he did for you. Tell what he did for sinners. That is all. "He shall glorify me: for he shall receive of mine, and shall shew it unto you."

I will not say more on this point, except that, if any of us are to glorify Christ, we must talk much of him. We must tell what the Holy Spirit has told to us; and we must pray the Holy Spirit to bless to the minds of men the truth we speak, by enabling them to see Christ as the Spirit reveals him.

But now, thirdly, in both of these things—showing unto us the things of Christ, and glorifying Christ—, THE HOLY SPIRIT IS A COMFORTER. Gracious Spirit, be a Comforter now to some poor struggling ones, by showing them the things of Christ, and by glorifying him in their salvation!

First, in showing to men the things of Christ, the Holy Spirit is a Comforter. *There is no comfort like a sight of Christ.* Sinner, your only comfort must lie in your Saviour, in his precious blood, and in his resurrection from the dead. Look that way, man! If you look inside, you will never find any comfort there. Look where the Holy Ghost looks. "He shall receive of mine, and shall shew it unto you." When a thing is shown to you, it is meant for you to look at it. If you want real comfort, I will tell you where to look, namely, to the person and work of the Lord Jesus Christ. "Oh!" say you, "but I am a wretched sinner." I know you are. You are a great deal worse than you think you are. "Oh, but I think myself the worst that ever lived." Yes, you are worse than that! You do not know half your depravity. You are worse than you ever dreamed that you were. But that is not where to look for comfort. "I am brutish," says one; "I am proud; I am self-righteous; I am envious; I have everything in me that is bad, sir, and if I have a little bit that is good sometimes, it is gone before I can see it. I am just lost, ruined, and undone." That is quite true; but I never told you to look there. Your comfort lies in this, "He shall receive of mine,"—that is, of Christ's,—"and shall shew it unto you." Your hope of transformation, of gaining a new character altogether, of eternal life, lies in Christ, who quickeneth the dead, and maketh all things new. Look away from self, and look to Christ, for he alone can save you.

A sight of Christ is the destruction of despair. "Oh, but the devil tells me that I shall be cast into hell! There is no hope for me." What matters it what the devil tells you? He was a liar from the beginning. Let him say what he likes; but if you will look away to Christ, there will be an end of the devil's power over you. If the Holy Ghost shows you what Christ came to do on the cross, and what he is doing on his throne in heaven, there will be an end to these troublous thoughts from Satan, and you will be comforted.

Dear child of God, are you *in sorrow now*? May the Holy Ghost take of the things of Christ, and show them unto you! There is an end to sorrow when you see Jesus, for sorrow itself is so sweetly sanctified by the companionship of Christ which it brings to you, that you will be glad to drink of his cup and to be baptized with his baptism.

Are you *in want*, without even a place where to lay your head? So, too, was he. "The Son of man hath not where to lay his head." Go to him with your trouble. He will help you to bear your poverty. He will help you to get out of it, for he is able to help you in temporal trials as well as in spiritual ones. Therefore go you to Christ. All power is given unto him in heaven and in earth. Nothing is too hard for the Lord. Go your way to him, and a sight of him will give you comfort.

Are you *persecuted*? Well, a sight of the thorn-crowned brow will take the thorn out of persecution. Are you very, very low? I think that you have all heard the story I am about to tell you, but some of you have, perhaps, forgotten it. Many years ago, when this great congregation first met in the Surrey Music Hall, and the terrible accident occurred when many persons were either killed or wounded in the panic, I did my best to hold the people together till I heard that some were dead, and then I broke down like a man stunned, and for a fortnight or so I had little reason left. I felt so broken in heart that I thought that I should never be able to face a congregation again; and I went down to a friend's house, a few miles away, to be very quiet and still. I was walking round his garden, and I well remember the spot, and even the time, when this passage came to me, "Him hath God exalted with his right hand to be a Prince and a Saviour;" and this thought came into my mind at once, "You are only a soldier in the great King's army, and you may die in a ditch; but it does not matter what becomes of you as long as your King is exalted. *He*—HE is glorious. God hath highly exalted him." You have heard of the old French soldiers when they lay a-dying. If the emperor came by, when they were ready to expire, they would just raise themselves up, and gave one more cheer for their beloved leader. *"Vive l'Empereur!"* would be their dying words. And so I just thought, *"He* is exalted. What matters it about me?" and in a moment my reason was perfectly restored. I was as clear as possible. I went into the house, had family prayer, and came back to preach to my congregation on the following Sabbath, restored only by having looked to Jesus, and having seen that he was glorious. If he is to the front, what does it matter what happens to us?

But now, lastly, *when Christ is glorified in the heart, he acts as a Comforter, too.* I believe that we should not have half the trouble that we have if we thought more of Christ. The fact is, that we think so much of ourselves that we get troubled. But someone says, "But I have so many troubles." Why should you not have a great many troubles? Who are you that you should not have troubles? "Oh, but I have had loss after loss which you do not know of!" Very likely. I do not know of your losses, but is it any wonder that you should have them? "Oh!" says one, "I seem to be kicked about like a football." Why should you not be? What are you? "Oh!" said one poor penitent to me the other night, "for me to come to Christ, sir, after my past life, seems so mean." I said, "Yes, so it is; but, then, you *are* mean. It was a mean business of the prodigal son to come home, and eat his father's bread and the fatted calf after he had spent his substance in riotous living." It was a mean thing, was it not? But, then, the father did not think it mean. He clasped him to his bosom, and welcomed him home. Come along, you mean sinners, you that have served the devil, and now want to run away from him! Steal away from Satan at once, for my Lord is ready to receive you. You have no idea how willing he is to welcome you. He is so ready to forgive, that you have not yet guessed how much sin he can forgive. "All manner of sin and blasphemy shall be forgiven unto men." Up to your necks in filth, in your very hearts saturated with the foulest iniquity; yet, if you come to Christ, he will wash you whiter than snow.

Have exalted ideas of Christ. Oh, if a man will but have great thoughts of Christ, he shall then find his troubles lessening, and

67

his sins disappearing! You have been putting Christ on a wrong scale altogether, I see. Perhaps even you people of God have not thought of Christ as you ought to do. I have heard of a certain commander who had led his troops into a rather difficult position. He knew what he was at, but the soldiers did not all know; and there would be a battle on the morrow. So he thought that he would go round from tent to tent, and hear what the soldiers said. He listened, and there was one of them saying to his fellows, "See what a mess we are in now! Do you see, we have only so many cavalry, and so many infantry, and we have only a small quantity of artillery. And on the other side there are so many thousands against us, so strong, so mighty, that we shall be cut to pieces in the morning." And the general drew aside the canvas, and there they saw him standing, and he said, "How many do you count *me* for?" He had won every battle that he had ever been engaged in. He was the conqueror of conquerors. "How many do you count me for?" O souls, you have never counted Christ for what he is! You have put down your sins, but you have never counted what kind of a Christ he is who has come to save you. Rather do like Luther, who says that, when the devil came to him, he brought him a long sheet containing a list of his sins, or of a great number of them, and Luther said to him, "Is that all?" "No," said the devil. "Well, go and fetch some more, then." Away went Satan to bring him another long list, as long as your arm. Said Luther, "Is that all?" "Oh, no!" said the devil, "I have more yet." "Well, go and bring them all," said Luther. "Fetch them all out, the whole list of them." Then it was a very long black list. I think that I have heard that it would have gone round the world twice. I know that mine would. Well, what did Luther say when he saw them all? He said, "Write at the bottom of them, 'The blood of Jesus Christ his Son cleanseth us from all sin!'" It does not matter how long the list is when you write those blessed words at the end of it. The sins are all gone then. So, though your sins are very many,—if you have trusted Jesus,—your sins are all gone, drowned in the Red Sea of your Saviour's blood, and Christ is glorified in your salvation. May God the Holy Ghost bring every unsaved one here to repentance and faith in our Lord Jesus Christ! The Lord bless every one of you, for his name's sake!

6

HARVEST PAST, AND MEN UNSAVED

"The harvest is past, the summer is ended, and we are not saved."—Jer. 8: 20.

THIS is a very mournful chapter, especially if we include in it, as we rightly should, the first verse of the ninth chapter: "Oh that my head were waters." The passage is full of lamentation and woe, and yet it is somewhat singular that the chief mourner here is not one who needed chiefly to be in trouble. Jeremiah was under the especial protection of God, and he escaped in the evil day. Even when Nebuchadnezzar was exercising his utmost rage, Jeremiah was in no danger, for the heart of the fierce monarch was kindly towards him. "Now Nebuchadnezzar king of Babylon gave charge concerning Jeremiah to Nebuzar-adan the captain of the guard, saying, take him, and look well to him, and do him no harm; but do unto him even as he shall say unto thee."

The man of God, who personally had least cause to mourn, was filled with heavy grief, while the people who were about to lose their all, and to lose their lives, still remained but half awakened; complaining, but not repenting; afraid, but yet not humbled before God. None of them uttered such a grievous lament as that which came from the heart and mouth of the prophet. Their heads were full of idle dreams, while his had become waters; their eyes were full of wantonness, while his were a fountain of tears. He loved them better than they loved themselves. Is it not strange that it should be so, that the physician should be more anxious than the sick man? Perhaps, however, it is not so singular that the shepherd should care more for the flock than the sheep care for themselves. When the sheep are men it is certainly an unreasonable thing! The weeping prophet cries, "For the hurt of the daughter of my people am I hurt;" he was more hurt than they were.

A preacher whom God sends will often feel more care for the souls of men than men feel for themselves or their own salvation. Is it not sad that there should be an anxious pain in the heart of one who is himself saved, while those who are unsaved, and are obliged to own it, feel little or no concern? To see a man in jeopardy of his life, and all around him alarmed for his danger, while he himself is half asleep, is a sad sight. See yonder man about to be condemned to die, standing at the bar, the judge putting on the black cap is scarcely able to pronounce the sentence for emotion, and all around him in the court break down with distress on his account, while he himself is brazen-faced and feels no more than the floor he stands upon! How hardened has he become! Pity is lost upon him, if pity ever can be lost.

Such a sad sight we constantly see in our congregations: those who are "condemned already" on account of sin are altogether indifferent to their awful peril, while their godly parents are greatly distressed for them, Christian people are pleading with them, and earnest messengers from God expostulating with them. Heaven and earth are moved for them, and yet they are unaffected. May none of you be hardened through the deceitfulness of sin. May God of his infinite mercy strike the rock, and make the waters of penitence to gush out from it. May his transforming hand turn stone into flesh, and cause a holy tenderness to banish all stubbornness and insensibility. Such is my agonising cry to the Holy Spirit.

Certainly there ought to be dismay, and even terror, in the heart of any who are compelled to use my text in reference to themselves. Those few words, "We are not saved!" sound like a peal of thunder. They should cut the soul as with a case of knives—"We are not saved!" What worse thing can men say of themselves? We are now under the abiding wrath of God, for "we are not saved!" We must soon stand before the judgment seat of God, and then we shall be condemned of the great Judge, for "we are not saved!" We shall ere long be driven from his Presence and from the glory of his power, for "we are not saved!" We shall then be shut out in outer darkness, where shall be weeping and wailing and gnashing of teeth, for "we are not saved!" Had men but reason, or having reason would they but use it upon the most important of all subjects, surely they would cry out in the bitterness of their souls, "Oh that our heads were water and our eyes fountains of tears, that we might weep day and night till we had found our Saviour and he had washed away our sin and saved us." How saddening to see the loaded waggons of harvest bearing no real blessing to us, and to watch the clusters on the vine ripen all unblessed! Alas for that summer which amid all its flowers yields us no perfume of peace or joy. On the other hand, how blessed to feel that the harvest is past, and the summer is ended, and blessed by God we are saved! Now let winter come with all its blasts, we have nothing to fear, for wrapped in our Saviour's righteousness, and hidden in the cleft of his side, we shall outlive every storm.

I earnestly pray the Lord to bless the words I am about to speak, that they may be rendered useful to many undecided persons to lead them to decision, and induce them to give themselves up to Christ at once. May the Holy Spirit work this blessed result in thousands. I have so long been silent that I am hungering to speak with power. Come Holy Spirit! Come!

First, I shall look at the text as *a complaint*—"We are not saved;" and, secondly, I shall suggest that out of it ought to come *consideration:* those who utter the complaint should be led thereby to solemn consideration.

First, we have before us the language of COMPLAINT. These Jews said, "The seasons are going by, the year is spending itself, the harvest is past, the vintage also is ended, and yet we are not saved." Some of them were captives in Babylon, and they fondly expected to be brought back from the distant land, but they were disappointed. They hoped that when the produce of the Nile had been reaped Egyptian troops would march against Nebuchadnezzar and break his power. Others of them had fled into the defenced cities, and taken refuge behind the walls of Jerusalem, and they also dreamed that the march of the Chaldeans would be stopped, and the land would be delivered from their invasion as soon as the summer heats were over. The rescue did not come; indeed, they could from Jerusalem hear the neighing of the Babylonian horses: "The snorting of his horses was heard from Dan: the whole land trembled at the sound of the neighing of his strong ones; for they are come, and have devoured the land, and all that is in it;

the city, and those that dwell therein." Therefore they complained that their hopes had failed. In effect they complained of God that he had not saved them, as if he was under some obligation to have done so, as if they had a kind of claim upon him to interpose: and so they spoke as if they were an ill-used people, a nation that had been neglected by their Protector. Husbandmen had gathered in the harvest, and vine-dressers had gleaned the grapes, yet they had not been cared for, but left to suffer: despite their hopes they were not saved. Certain persons fall into the same state of mind in these days. They know that they are not saved, but they do not blame themselves for it; they would not like to say where it does lie, but they will not own that it lies in themselves. They are not saved, and somebody should be blamed for it, or perhaps nobody, but they mention the fact, not as a confession of which they are ashamed, but as a misfortune for which they are to be pitied.

This complaint was a very unjust one, for there were many reasons why they were not saved and why God had not delivered them.

The first was *they had looked to the wrong quarter:* they expected that the Egyptians would deliver them. You remember that in the reign of Zedekiah the Jews revolted from their subjection to the Babylonians because they hoped that the king of Egypt would come up and fight with the Babylonian power. Those who were captives hoped that yet the great armies of the Pharaohs might break down the might of Chaldea, and so they looked to Egypt for help, an old fault with Israel and a gross folly, for why should they look to the house of bondage for succour? The same folly dwells in multitudes of men. They are not saved, and they never will be while they continue to look where they do look. All dependence upon ourselves is looking to Egypt for help, and leaning our weight upon a broken reed. Whether that dependence upon self takes the form of relying upon ceremonies, or depending upon prayers, or trusting in our own attempts to improve ourselves morally, it is still the same proud folly of self-dependence. Vain is all searching for legal righteousness, hoping to merit something of God, or to do something without help from on high, for the Lord himself has assured us that by the works of the law no flesh shall be justified. You may have been very earnest and serious about divine things, but if you have looked in any measure or degree to what you are, or can do, or what any man can do for you, it is no wonder that you are not saved, for there is no salvation there.

I am afraid some think that it is a great thing to sit under a faithful minister, that if the gospel be thoroughly preached they may naturally expect that if they take a seat at the place they will be saved. But all dependence upon ministers is only another form of superstitious confidence in priestcraft. All trust but that which is found in Jesus is a delusion and a falsehood. No man can help you. Though Noah, Samuel, and Moses prayed for you, their prayers could not avail unless you believed in the blood of Jesus; there is salvation nowhere else. Though the whole church were to unite in one protracted intercession, and determine that all its ministers should preach to you alone for the next seven years, there would be no more hope of your being saved then than now, unless you would believe in the Lord Jesus Christ, who alone is the salvation of the sons of men. The most fruitful of harvests may pass and the most genial of summers may smile upon you, but while you look to yourself no sunshine from God shall cause you to flourish. Eternal barrenness is the portion of those who trust in man and make flesh their arm. While men go about to establish their own righteousness, and will not submit themselves to the righteousness of Christ, they shall be like the woman who spent all her living upon physicians, and was nothing better, but rather grew worse.

Those people had *prided themselves upon their outward privileges;* they had presumed upon their favoured position, for they say in the nineteenth verse, "Is not the Lord in Zion? is not her king in her?" Because they belonged to the chosen nation, because the Lord had entrusted them with the sacred oracles, and manifested himself to their fathers, therefore they thought that they might sin with impunity, and reckon upon being delivered in the day of danger. I do not know how many of you here may be depending upon outward religiousness, or indulging some kind of thought that, apart from your personal faith in Christ, you will be saved by your pious connections and hallowed relationships; but if that is what you are depending upon, rest assured you will be deceived. Vain are the baptism or the

73

confirmation of your youth: faith in Jesus is the one thing needful; vain is the fact that you were born of Christian parents: ye must be born again; vain is your sitting as God's people sit, and standing as they stand, in the solemn service of the sanctuary: your heart must be changed; vain is your observance of the Lord's Day, and vain your Bible reading and your form of prayer night and morning, unless you are washed in Jesus' blood; vain are all things without living faith in the living Jesus. Though you had been descended from an unbroken line of saints, though you had no unconverted relative, your ancestry and lineage would not avail you; the sons of God are born, not of blood, nor of the will of man, nor of the will of the flesh, but of God. All the external privileges that can be heaped upon you, though you had sermons piled up and Gospel services heaped on them, as the giants piled mountain upon mountain, Pelion upon Ossa, that they might climb to heaven, would be useless; there is no reaching to salvation by such means. If your reliance be upon external ordinances, of professions or privileges in any measure or degree, no wonder that the harvest is past, and the summer is ended, and you are not saved, for you never will be saved till doomsday while you look in that direction. Look like sinners to your Saviour and you shall be saved, but not else.

Thirdly, there was another and very powerful reason why these people were not saved, for, with all their religiousness and their national boast as to God's being among them, they *had continued in provoking the Lord*. He says in the nineteenth verse, "Why have they provoked me to anger with their graven images and with strange vanities?" They lived in sin, disobeying God to his face; they set up new idols, and imported false deities from foreign lands, and yet they said, "We are not saved." Would they have the Lord sanction their degrading idolatry by sending them deliverance? Do you know a man who goes frequently into ill company, and gets intoxicated, and yet comes to hear the gospel, and murmurs that he is not saved? Is he not mad? Let me speak plainly to him. Do you think that you are going to heaven to reel about the holy streets? Shall the pure heavens be polluted by your profanities? You are dreadfully mistaken if you fancy so. Another person indulges lust, lives an unclean life, and yet he comes in and listens to the word of God as one who has a loving ear for it, and he also complains that he is not saved. O unclean man, how canst thou dream of salvation whilst thou art defiled with filthiness? What, thou and thy harlot, members of Christ! Oh, thou knowest not my pure and holy Master. He receiveth sinners, but he rejecteth those who delight in their iniquities. Thou must have done with the indulgence of sin if thou wouldst be cleansed from the guilt of it. There is no going on in transgression, and yet obtaining salvation: it is a licentious supposition. Christ comes to save us from our sins, not to make it safe to do evil. That blood which washes out the stain brings with it also a hatred of the thing which made the stain. Sin must be relinquished, or salvation cannot be received.

I spoke very plainly just now, but some here of pure heart little know how plainly we must speak if we are to reach some men's consciences, for it shames me when I think of some who year after year indulge in secret sin, and yet they are regular frequenters of the house of God. You would think they surely were already converted, or soon would be when you saw them here, but if you followed them home you would quite despair of them. O lovers of sin do not deceive yourselves, you will surely reap that which you sow. How can grace reign in you while you are the slaves of your own passions? How can it be while you are anchored to a secret sin that you should be borne along by the current of grace towards the desired haven of safety? Either you must leave your sin or leave all hope of heaven; if you hold your sin hell will ere long hold you. Jesus was not sent to be the minister of sin; he never came into the world to bleed and die to make the way of the transgressors easy by enabling them to be vicious without risk. The friend of sinners is the enemy of sin. There is a religion that will let you pay a shilling or two and purchase priestly absolution, but this we protest against. Such a faith may well breed iniquity. What can it be but like Egypt's Nile, when in the days of Moses it became the fruitful mother of ten thousand unclean frogs? Under the religion of Christ absolution for the past is only to be obtained through faith in Jesus, and that faith brings with it repentance for former offences, and a change of life for days to come. Wherefore do men say "We are not saved" when they are still hugging their iniquities? They may as well hope to gather grapes of thorns or figs of thistles, as to find salvation while they abide in sin. May God deliver us all from the love of sin, for such a deliverance is salvation.

Again, there was another reason why they were not saved, and that was because *they made being saved from trouble the principal matter*. Many make a great mistake about salvation; they mistake the meaning of the term, and to them salvation means being delivered from going down into the pit of hell, just as to these Jews it meant rescue from Nebuchadnezzar. Now, the right meaning of salvation is purification from evil. These people never thought of this: they never said, "We are not cleansed, we are not made holy," but "we are not saved." If their cry had been, "The harvest is past, the summer is ended, and we have not yet conquered sin," that would have been a mark of something good and true, but they showed no trace of it. There is not much in a man's desiring to be saved if he means by that an escape from the punishment of his offences. Was there ever a murderer yet who did not wish to be saved from the gallows? When a man is tied up to be flogged for a deed of brutal violence, and his back is bared for the lash, depend upon it he repents of what he did; that is to say, he repents that he has to suffer for it; but that is all, and a sorry all too. He has no sorrow for the agony which he inflicted on his innocent victim; no regret for maiming him for life.

What is the value of such a repentance? Here is the point: do you wish to have new hearts? If you do you shall have them. Do you wish to leave the sins you have loved? Do you desire to live as Christ lived? Do you wish to keep the commandments of God? Do you sigh for purity of life? Do you wish henceforth to be as God would have you to be, just, loving, kind, chaste, after the example of the great Redeemer? If so, then truly the desire you have cometh of God; but if all you want is to be able to die without dread, that you may wake up in the next world and not be driven down to the bottomless pit, if that is all, there is nothing gracious in it, and it is no wonder that you should say, "The harvest is past, the summer is ended, and I am not saved." You do not know what being saved means. God teach you to love holiness, and there shall not pass another harvest, nay not another day, before you shall be saved; indeed, that very love is the dawn of salvation. Seek salvation as the kingdom of God within you, seek it first and seek it now, and you shall not be denied.

Again, there was another reason why these people were not saved and could not be. Read the ninth verse, and see their fault and folly: "Lo, *they have rejected the word of the Lord,* and what wisdom is in them?" We hear persons complain that they are not saved, though they neglect the saving word. They go to a place of worship and therefore wonder that they are not saved; how can they be when that which they hear is not the object of their heart's attention? Do you read your Bible privately? Did you ever read it with an earnest prayer that God would teach you what you really are, and make you to be a true believer in Christ? Have you done that just as earnestly as you studied a book when you were trying to pass an examination? I do not know what calling you follow, but I will suppose, for instance, that you wish to be a chemist; if so, you go through a course of studies, and you acquaint yourself with certain books, in order that you may pass an examination. You stick to your work, for you know that you will not pass unless you are well informed as to the matters needful to your profession. Do you show the same diligence in reference to your soul and your God? Have you ever read your Bible with anything like the same intensity with which a man must study a class-book in order to pass his examinations? Have you read it with regard to yourself, asking God to teach you its meaning, and to make the sense of it press upon your conscience? Do you reply, "I have not done that"? Why then do you wonder that you are not saved? To put a slighter test than the former: when you hear the Gospel, do you always enquire, "What has this to do with me?" or do you listen to it as a general truth with which you have no peculiar concern?

What a difference is perceptible in hearers! Numbers of persons have come hither at this time merely to hear Spurgeon preach, and form an estimate of him. Is this a fit errand for God's day, and for an assembly gathered for worship? Do not imagine that we are flattered by such attentions. We do not covet such hearers. What care I about their estimate? A poor soul that wants to find Christ is a diamond in my eyes, but he who comes to hear me because of public talk is a common pebble that one might sling away, only it is well that even he

77

should hear the word if perchance God might bless him. Many of you Christian people hear sermons that you may remember well-turned sentences and pithy sayings, or that you may gauge the preacher's earnestness, and judge whether he is likely to be useful. Hearing for others is a very common amusement. There is a deal of difference between walking through a baker's shop when you are well filled and counting all the loaves upon the shelves, and rushing in at the door to get a bit of bread at once, for fear of dying of starvation. Water seen as a picturesque object by a traveller is one thing, but a living draught swallowed by one dying of thirst is quite a different matter.

O that men would treat the Gospel as a necessary of life, which they must each one feed upon or perish. That is the style of hearing when a man prays that the word of God may search him, and try him. It is well when the hearer bares his bosom and cries, "Lord cut this cancer out of my soul, I pray thee. I beseech thee, let me live!" That kind of hearing ends in saving. "Incline your ear," saith the great Lord, "and come unto me; hear, and your soul shall live" (Isa. 55:3). "Hearken diligently unto me," saith he again; and in so doing he certifies that diligent hearkening shall bring a blessing with it. Alas, with the bulk of hearers the word goes in at one ear and out at the other. The noise of God's voice is drowned by the din of the world's traffic, the six days crush the influence of the seventh, and it is no wonder that January comes and December goes, and yet worldlings are not saved. They never will be while they slumber as they do.

There is a further reason why some men are not saved, and that is because *they have a great preference for slight measures*. They love to hear the flattering voice whispering—"Peace, peace, where there is no peace"; and they choose those for leaders who will heal their hurt slightly. They wish for something very comfortable, and in their folly they prefer poisoned sweets to healthful salts. "I felt so miserable," said one, "when I left that place that I said I would never enter it again." It was a foolish vow. He who is wise will go where the word has most power, both to kill and to make alive. Do you want a physician when you call upon him to please you with a flattering opinion? Must he needs say, "My dear friend, it is a very small matter; you want nothing but pleasant diet, and you will soon be all right"? If he talks thus smoothly when he knows that a deadly disease is commencing its work upon you, is he not a deceiver? Do you not think you are very foolish if you pay such a man your guinea, and denounce his neighbour who tells you the plain truth? Do you want to be deluded? Are you eager to be duped? Do you want to dream of heaven, and then wake up in hell? Have I such an idiot here? May heaven save him from his ruinous folly.

For my part, I should like to know the worst of my case, and things must be very bad with any one of you who cannot say the same. When a merchant dares not face his books, you know where he is. When he says to his clerk, "No, no, I do not want to know on which side the balance stands. I cannot bear to be worried. I dare say money will come in as well as go out, and my credit will raise me another loan. Things will come round, and the less we dive into difficulties the better." We shall hear of that gentleman very speedily in the Bankruptcy Court, I think. He is in the same condition spiritually who does not dare to face himself, but would rather not be troubled with questions and examinations. What, dare you not look yourself in the face? Have you covered up the looking-glass? Have you hid the word of God from yourselves, and dare not see how you look? Ay, then be sure you are in an evil plight. While men will not have the thorough-going truth preached to them, while they like some siren strain, while they would fain listen to soft music and float upon gentle streams that bear them down to destruction, there is little hope but what harvests and summers will come and go, and they will not be saved.

All this while these people have wondered that they were not saved, and yet *they never repented of their sin*. The Lord himself witnesses against them, "I hearkened and heard, but they spake not aright: no man repented him of his wickedness, saying, What have I done? Every one turned to his course, as the horse rusheth into the battle." "Were they ashamed when they had committed abomination? Nay, they were not at all ashamed, neither could they blush." Repentance was a jest with them, they had not grace enough even to feel shame, and yet they made a complaint against God, saying, "The harvest is past, the summer is ended, and we are not saved." What monstrous folly was this! Where has the Lord given half a promise to those who will **not** confess and forsake their **sins?** How can impenitent sinners hope that they should be forgiven?

We have said enough upon this unjustifiable complaint. Now, may the Spirit of God help us while we would lead unconverted persons into the CONSIDERATION of this matter.

First consideration, *"we are not saved."* I do not want to talk, I want you to think. "We are not saved." Put it in the personal, first person singular. Will everyone here only do me the favour of saying that to himself if it is true, "I am not saved! I am not saved! I am not saved from sin, I love it still. I am not saved from guilt, I am condemned for my failure to keep the law. I am not saved from wrath, I am not saved from judgment, I am not saved from the eternal curse. I am not saved! My dear child in heaven is for ever happy, but I am not saved. My dear wife is a happy Christian, but I am not saved. I am one of a family where many have been converted, but I am not saved. I am a grey-headed old man, and I am not saved. I am beloved in my family by my dear mother, for I am yet a child, but though she prays for me I am not saved." "I am a member of a church and am not saved." Are you obliged to say that, any of you? Be honest, then. Do not cover up the truth, however terrible it may be; better far to face it. What if some one must confess, "I am a preacher of the Gospel, but I am not saved." Oh, my heart, what terror is here! It is an awful thing if anybody here has to say, "I am a teacher in a Sunday School, and this afternoon the little ones will gather round me, but I am not saved. People respect me, they say I have all things good about me, but I have not the one thing needful, I am not saved." Teachers, does this touch any one of you? I pray you let it have its due influence. Now you down here in the area, and you in these galleries, will you do one of the two things; either say "By God's grace I have believed in Jesus and I am saved," or else just sigh out silently in your soul, "I am not saved." It will do you good to end all questions, and know once for all whether you are in Christ or not.

Furthermore, not only am I not saved, but *I have been a long time not saved.* Let me put language into the mouths of those who are ruining themselves by delay. "Time flies. How quickly it is gone! I was a young man a very little while ago, now I am getting into middle age, getting a little bald, grey hairs are upon me here and there. Why, dear me, here are grandchildren come—it seems but yesterday that I was married. Yes, harvests have passed, vintages have been gathered, and I am not saved. Twenty years ago I sat listening to this same preacher, and I was not saved then; and I remember how he touched my conscience, but all those years have gone, and I am not saved. The world has had its opportunities and used them; they sowed and they reaped their harvests. The vine-dresser used the knife and the vine was pruned, and in due season he gathered the clusters, but I have had no harvest, I have known no vintage. I have made money, I have got on in business, or at least I have just paid my way and supported my family, but I have had no spiritual harvest; no, for I never sowed. I have had no spiritual vintage, for I was never pruned. I never went to the great Husbandman and asked him to dig about me and make me fruitful to his name. What opportunities I had! I have been through revivals, but the sacred power passed over me; I remember several wonderful occasions when the Spirit of God was poured out, and yet I am not saved."

Worse still, *habits harden.* "If I was not saved during the last twenty or thirty years I am less likely to be impressed now. I do not feel as I once did. Sometimes the vile unbelief which now taints the very air creeps over me, and I am half a sceptic. Considerations that used to thrill me, and make my flesh creep, are now put before me, but I seem like a piece of steel—nay, I do not even rust under the word, I am unimpressible. Harvests have dried me, summers have parched me, age has shrivelled my soul: my moisture is turned into the drought of summer, I am getting to be old hay, or as withered weeds fit for the burning." It is a dreadful consideration for a man to turn over in his mind, but it is a very needful one, for it is an undoubted fact that every year fixes the character and engraves the lines of evil deeper in the nature. Harvests and summers leave us worse if they do not see us mend. As true as you are alive, unless God of infinite mercy arouse you out of your present condition to seek and immediately find Christ, and obtain everlasting life, some of you will settle down into a condition which will be the eternal state of your hearts. O for grace to repent at once, ere yet the wax has cooled and the seal is set for ever.

The last summer will soon come, and the last harvest will soon be reaped, and you must go to your long home. I will apply it mainly to myself: I must go up stairs for the last time, and I must lay me down upon the bed from which I shall never rise again; if I am unsaved my room will be a prison chamber to me, and the bed will be hard as a plank, if I have to lie there and know that I must die, that a few more days or hours must end this struggle for existence, and I am bound to stand before God. O my God, save me from an unready death-bed! Save these people from dying and passing into hell! You will have no doubts about it then, you know; you will see clearly that you are bound to stand before God. This naked spirit of mine, disrobed of its body, must appear before the Judge! What shall I do? What shall I say? Before my Maker's burning eyes, stripped naked to my shame, oh! what shall I do? And when I speechless stand before him, by my silence owning to my guilt, what shall I do? The gate of heaven is shut, I cannot enter there. I have not the password; I have rejected the way thither; I have rejected Christ, who is the King of the place; oh! whither must I go? I will not paint the picture. Souls, I charge you by everything that is rational within you, escape for your lives, and seek to find eternal salvation for your undying spirits. You are not dogs nor cats, nor horses nor cattle, as men tell you; you are nobler things, and an immortality awaits you, and you shall make to-day that immortality the most awful curse that can fall upon you, or a privilege infinite, unutterable. It is a grand alternative. God help us by his infinite mercy to choose eternal holiness and everlasting joy, and choose it now.

Come, let us consider a little longer a few practical truths which may be of service. It is quite clear that, if you are to get right, you must not go on in the old way. The harvest is past, and the summer is ended, and by the way in which you have been going on you are not saved. There must be a change of tactics. Salvation must be thought of in another light, and sought for in another spirit. Come, if you are to find salvation you must be more earnest about it, you must be more intense about it; there must be a greater valuing of this salvation, and a more solemn resolve that if heaven or earth or hell can yield it to you, you will have it, for "the kingdom of heaven suffereth violence, and the violent take it by force" (Matt. 11: 12). Never did a man sleep himself into eternal life. Salvation is all of grace, but sluggards have no grace. The Lord does not work in us to sleep and to slumber, but to will and to do. Men reach the Celestial City, not by drowsiness, but by their spirits being stirred to feel that there is nothing else that is worth a thought compared with going on pilgrimage to glory.

There is one thing certain, that, as the harvests have past and the summer is ended and we have not been saved, we must have been looking in the wrong place. Very likely we have been looking to something on earth for salvation. If so, we have not found it, because it is not there. The prophet enquires: "Is there no balm in Gilead: is there no physician there?" (Jer. 8: 22). He knew that there was none in that region which could meet his people's dreadful hurt. There was a balm in Gilead, but it was the resin of a tree; there were physicians there, but they were mostly quacks that duped the people. If there had been any true balm and any real physician there, the health of the daughter of his people would have been recovered. No, there is "no balm in Gilead" for you. The "balm of Gilead" was only good for certain bodily wounds and sores, but not for cuts and wounds and sores like these, for these are in the soul. The physicians of Gilead could only heal some few complaints, and seldom enough did they heal even these, but all the physicians of Gilead in a row cannot heal *your complaint*. I will tell you of another and better health-resort than Gilead—it is Calvary. Where Jesus bled you will find a balm; where Jesus lives you will find a physician.

Another thing must have suggested itself to you while I have been preaching, if you have listened in earnest; and it is this, that the great point must be that if I am to be saved *I must get rid of sin*. I will again speak for those whom I address. "I have been thinking that I should undergo some strange transformation, and some kind of mysterious shock, or have a vision or see some strange sight, and that then I should say I am a converted man. I discover that the main point is to get rid of sin; it must be driven out of my heart. I have not only to leave off the act of it, and the thought of it, but all love to it must go. I cannot be a saved man unless that is the case." If you have kept pace with the preacher so far, I think the next thought will come: "Then this is deep water; this is a place where my own strength utterly fails me. If I must have a new heart—well, I cannot make myself a new heart. If the very love of sin has to go, I cannot accomplish that; I can stop outside the theatre, but I cannot prevent my wanting to go in. I can renounce dishonesty, but I cannot help having an itching palm. Even if I dare not transgress yet I may feel the wish to do so if the punishment could be escaped.

This makes the matter too hard for unaided nature; since it is true that unless the love of sin is gone nothing is done. God must help me, or this will never be accomplished. This is the centre of the truth. Your great Creator must come and make you over again. His dear Son must come and end your captivity to the power of evil. He has come, he has died. Nothing can ever take out the stains of your past sin but the blood of the Son of God. Nothing can take from you the love of sin but the application of the atoning blood, and the work of the Spirit upon your entire nature, creating you anew in Christ Jesus. "Oh," saith one, "I see it all now. I seem to have come up against a wall of rock, and I can go no further. I wonder not that the summers have gone and the harvests have ended, when it is like this; for now I am brought up before a dread impossibility. What can I do?" Thou canst do this. God helping you, trust Christ to do it all. Throw thyself down at his feet. "Saviour, Saviour, from the highest heaven look down, here is a sinner in his blood. I read of others that when they were in their blood thou saidst to them, Live! Say that to me. Here is one condemned, and near to die; save him, forgive him, impute thy righteousness, make me to be accepted in the Beloved. I trust thee!"

Do you indeed trust Jesus? Is it true that you believe on him? Then you are saved! His merit is yours, his blood has cleansed you the moment you believe in him, it is done: you shall not love sin again. You shall be tempted, and often have to groan because of secret listings that will linger there; but you have a new life now, for you have believed in Jesus, and that new life will abhor sin, and will fight it, and will conquer it, and God will help you, and the Spirit will dwell in you, and you shall get sin more and more under your feet—yea, you shall bruise Satan under your feet ere long, and you shall triumph, and one day you shall burst this shell which holds you in, and you shall shine in the image of Christ, "without spot or wrinkle, or any such thing."

Yes, you, sinful man, shall be made perfectly holy, even you, now full of iniquity, transgression, and sin. You are a God-provoking rebel now, but if you trust in Christ Jesus you shall be washed and made God-pleasing this very day: black as hell to-day, you shall by infinite mercy be made as bright as a seraph before God, and all that because you trust the Saviour. O God, grant us thy saving grace for Jesus' sake.

7

"HE COMETH WITH CLOUDS"

"Behold, he cometh with clouds; and every eye shall see him, and they also which pierced him: and all kindreds of the earth shall wail because of him. Even so, Amen."—Rev. 1: 7.

IN reading the chapter we observed how the beloved John saluted the seven churches in Asia with, "Grace and peace be unto you." Blessed men scatter blessings. When the *benediction* of God rests on us we pour out benediction upon others.

From benediction John's gracious heart rose into *adoration* of the great King of Saints. As our hymn puts it, "The holy to the holiest leads." They that are good at blessing men will be quick at blessing God.

It is a wonderful doxology which John has given us: "Unto him that loved us, and washed us from our sins in his own blood, and hath made us kings and priests unto God and his Father; to him be glory and dominion for ever and ever. Amen." I like the Revised Version for its alliteration in this case, although I cannot prefer it for other reasons. It runs thus: "Unto him that *loveth* us, and *loosed* us from our sins by his blood." Truly our Redeemer has loosed us from sin; but the mention of his blood suggests washing rather than loosing. We can keep the alliteration and yet retain the meaning of cleansing if we read the passage, "Unto him that loved us, and laved us." *Loved* us, and *laved* us: carry those two words home with you: let them lie upon your tongue to sweeten your breath for prayer and praise. "Unto him that loved us, and laved us, be glory and dominion for ever and ever."

Then John tells of the dignity which the Lord hath put upon us in making us kings and priests, and from this he ascribes royalty and dominion unto the Lord himself. John had been extolling the Great King, whom he calls, "The Prince of the kings of the earth." Such indeed he was, and is, and is to be.

When John had touched upon that royalty which is natural to our divine Lord, and that dominion which has come to him by conquest, and by the gift of the Father as the reward of all his travail, he then went on to note that he has "made us kings." Our Lord's royalty he diffuses among his redeemed. We praise him because he is in himself a king, and next, because he is a King-maker, the Fountain of honour and majesty. He has not only enough of royalty for himself, but he hands a measure of his dignity to his people. He makes kings out of such common stuff as he finds in us poor sinners. Shall we not adore him for this? Shall we not cast our crowns at his feet? He gave our crowns to us; shall we not give them to him? "To him be glory and dominion for ever and ever. Amen." King by thy divine nature! King by filial right! King-maker, lifting up the beggar from the dunghill to set him among princes! King of kings by the unanimous love of all thy crownèd ones! Thou art he whom thy brethren shall praise! Reign thou for ever and ever! Unto thee be hosannas of welcome and hallelujahs of praise. Lord of the earth and heaven, let all things that be, or ever shall be, render unto thee all glory in the highest degree. Do not your souls take fire as you think of the praises of Immanuel? Fain would I fill the universe with his praise. Oh for a thousand tongues to sing the glories of the Lord Jesus! If the Spirit who dictated the words of John has taken possession of our spirits, we shall find adoration to be our highest delight. Never are we so near to heaven as when we are absorbed in the worship of Jesus, our Lord and God. Oh, that I could now adore him as I shall do when, delivered from this encumbering body, my soul shall behold him in the fulness of his glory!

It would seem from the chapter that the adoration of John was increased by his *expectation* of the Lord's second coming; for he cries, "Behold, he cometh with clouds." His adoration awoke his expectation, which all the while was lying in his soul as an element of that vehement heat of reverent love which he poured forth in his doxology. "Behold, he cometh," said he, and thus he revealed one source of his reverence. "Behold, he cometh," said he, and this exclamation was the result of his reverence. He adored until his faith realized his Lord, and became a second and nobler sight.

I think, too, that his reverence was deepened and his adoration was rendered more fervent by his conviction of the speediness of his Lord's coming. "Behold, he cometh," or is coming: he means to assert that he is even now on his way. As workmen are moved to be more diligent in service when they hear their master's footfall, so, doubtless, saints are quickened in their devotion when they are conscious that he whom they worship is drawing near. He has gone away to the Father for a while, and so he has left us alone in this world; but he has said, "I will come again and receive you unto myself," and we are confident that he will keep his word. Sweet is the remembrance of that loving promise. That assurance is pouring its savour into John's heart while he is adoring; and it becomes inevitable, as well as most meet and proper, that his doxology should at its close introduce him to the Lord himself, and cause him to cry out, "Behold, he cometh." Having worshipped among the pure in heart, he sees the Lord: having adored the King, he sees him assume the judgment-seat, and appear in the clouds of heaven. When once we enter upon heavenly things we know not how far we can go, nor how high we can climb. John who began with blessing the churches now beholds his Lord.

May the Holy Ghost help us reverently to think of the wondrous coming of our blessed Lord, when he shall appear to the delight of his people and the dismay of the ungodly!

There are three things in the text. They will seem commonplaces to some of you, and, indeed, they are the common-places of our divine faith, and yet nothing can be of greater importance. The first is, *our Lord Jesus comes:* "Behold he cometh with clouds." The second is, *our Lord Jesus Christ's coming will be seen of all:* "Every eye shall see him, and they also which pierced him." And, in the third place, *this coming will cause great sorrow:* "All kindreds of the earth shall wail because of him."

May the Holy Spirit help us while, in the first place, we remember that OUR LORD JESUS CHRIST COMES!

This announcement is thought worthy of a note of admiration. As the Latins would say, there is an "*Ecce*" placed here— "*Behold*, he cometh." As in the old books the printers put hands in the margin pointing to special passages, such is this "behold!" It is a *Nota Bene* calling upon us to note well what we are reading. Here is something which we are to *hold* and *behold*.

88

We now hear a voice crying, "Come and see!" The Holy Spirit never uses superfluous words, nor redundant notes of exclamation: when he cries, "Behold!" it is because there is reason for deep and lasting attention. Will you turn away when he bids you pause and ponder, linger and look? Oh, you that have been beholding vanity, come and behold the fact that Jesus cometh. You that have been beholding this, and beholding that, and thinking of nothing worthy of your thoughts; forget these passing sights and spectacles, and for once behold a scene which has no parallel. It is not a monarch in her jubilee, but the King of kings in his glory. That same Jesus who went up from Olivet into heaven is coming again to earth in like manner as his disciples saw him go up into heaven. Come and behold this great sight. If ever there was a thing in the world worth looking at, it is this. Behold and see if there was ever glory like unto his glory! Hearken to the midnight cry, "Behold, the bridegroom cometh!" It has practically to do with you. "Go ye forth to meet him." This voice is to you, O sons of men. Do not carelessly turn aside; for the Lord God himself demands your attention: he commands you to "Behold!" Will you be blind when God bids you behold? Will you shut your eyes when your Saviour cries, "Behold"? When the finger of inspiration points the way, will not your eye follow where it directs you? "Behold, he cometh." Look hither, I beseech you.

If we read the words of our text carefully, this "Behold" shows us first, that *this coming is to be vividly realized*. I think I see John. He is in the spirit; but on a sudden he seems startled into a keener and more solemn attention. His mind is more awake than usual, though he was ever a man of bright eyes that saw afar. We always liken him to the eagle for the height of his flight and the keenness of his vision; yet on a sudden, even he seems startled with a more astounding vision. He cries out, "Behold! Behold!" He has caught sight of his Lord. He says not, "He will come by-and-by," but, "I can see him; he is now coming." He has evidently realized the second advent. He has so conceived of the second coming of the Lord that it has become a matter of fact to him; a matter to be spoken of, and even to be written down.

"Behold, he cometh!" Have you and I ever realized the coming of Christ so fully as this? Perhaps we believe that he will come. I should hope that we all do *that*. If we believe that the Lord Jesus has come the first time, we believe also that he will come the second time; but are these equally assured truths to us? Peradventure we have vividly realized the first appearing: from Bethlehem to Golgotha, and from Calvary to Olivet we have traced the Lord, understanding that blessed cry, "Behold the Lamb of God, which taketh away the sin of the world!" Yes, the Word was made flesh and dwelt among us, and we beheld his glory, the glory as of the Only-begotten of the Father, full of grace and truth. But have we with equal firmness grasped the thought that he comes again without a sin-offering unto salvation? Do we now say to each other, as we meet in happy fellowship, "Yes, our Lord cometh"? It should be to us not only a prophecy assuredly believed among us, but a scene pictured in our souls, and anticipated in our hearts. My imagination has often set forth that dread scene: but better still, my faith has realized it. I have heard the chariot-wheels of the Lord's approach, and I have endeavoured to set my house in order for his reception. I have felt the shadow of that great cloud which shall attend him, damping the ardour of my worldliness. I hear even now in spirit the sound of the last trumpet, whose tremendous blast startles my soul to serious action, and puts force into my life. Would God that I lived more completely under the influence of that august event!

To this realization I invite you. I wish that we could go together in this, until as we went out of the house we said to one another, "Behold, he cometh!" One said to his fellow, after the Lord had risen, "The Lord has risen indeed." I want you to feel just as certain that the Lord is coming indeed, and I would have you say as much to one another. We are sure that he will come, and that he is on the way; but the benefit of a more vivid realization would be incalculable.

This coming is to be zealously proclaimed, for John does not merely calmly say, "He cometh," but he vigorously cries, "Behold, he cometh." Just as the herald of a king prefaces his message by a trumpet blast that calls attention, so John cries, "Behold!" As the old town-crier was wont to say, "O yes! O yes! O yes!" or to use some other striking formula by which he called upon men to note his announcement, so John stands in the midst of us, and cries, "Behold, he cometh!" He calls attention by that emphatic word "Behold!" It is no ordinary message that he brings, and he would not have us treat his word as a common-place saying. He throws his heart into the announcement. He proclaims it loudly, he proclaims it solemnly, and he proclaims it with authority: "Behold, he cometh."

No truth ought to be more frequently proclaimed, next to the first coming of the Lord, than his second coming; and you cannot thoroughly set forth all the ends and bearings of the first advent if you forget the second. At the Lord's Supper, there is no discerning the Lord's body unless you discern his first coming; but there is no drinking into his cup to its fulness, unless you hear him say, "Until I come." You must look forward, as well as backward. So must it be with all our ministries; they must look to him on the Cross and on the Throne. We must vividly realize that he, who has once come, is coming yet again, or else our testimony will be marred and one-sided. We shall make lame work of preaching and teaching if we leave out either advent.

And next, *it is to be unquestionably asserted*. "Behold, he cometh." It is not, "Perhaps he will come"; nor, "Peradventure he may yet appear." "Behold, he cometh" should be dogmatically asserted as an absolute certainty, which has been realized by the heart of the man who proclaims it. "Behold, he cometh." All the prophets say that he will come. From Enoch down to the last that spoke by inspiration, they declare, "The Lord cometh with ten thousands of his saints." You shall not find one who has spoken by the authority of God, who does not, either directly or by implication, assert the coming of the Son of man, when the multitudes born of woman shall be summoned to his bar, to receive the recompense of their deeds. All the promises are travailing with this prognostication, "Behold, he cometh." We have his own word for it, and this makes assurance doubly sure. He has told us that he will come again. He often assured his disciples that if he went away from them, he would come again to them; and he left us the Lord's Supper as a parting token to be observed until he comes. As often as we break bread we are reminded of the fact that, though it is a most blessed ordinance, yet it is a temporary one, and will cease to be celebrated when our absent Lord is once again present with us.

What is there to hinder Christ from coming? When I have studied and thought over this word, "Behold, he cometh," yes, I have said to myself, indeed he does; who shall hold him back? His heart is with his church on earth. In the place where he fought the battle he desires to celebrate the victory. His delights are with the sons of men. All his saints are waiting for the day of his appearing, and he is waiting also. The very earth in her sorrow and her groaning travaileth for his coming, which is to be her redemption. The creation is made subject to vanity for a little while; but, when the Lord shall come again, the creation itself also shall be delivered from the bondage of corruption into the glorious liberty of the children of God. We might question whether he would come a second time if he had not already come the first time; but, if he came to Bethlehem, be assured that his feet shall yet stand upon Olivet. If he came to die, doubt not that he will come to reign. If he came to be despised and rejected of men, why should we doubt that he will come to be admired in all them that believe? His sure coming is to be unquestionably asserted.

This fact that he will come again, *is to be taught as demanding our immediate interest*. "Behold, he cometh with clouds." Behold, look at it; meditate on it. It is worth thinking of. It concerns yourself. Study it again and again. "He cometh." He will so soon be here that it is put in the present tense: "He cometh." That shaking of the earth; that blotting out of sun and moon; that fleeing of heaven and earth before his face—all these are so nearly here that John describes them as accomplished. "Behold, he cometh."

There is this sense lying in the background, that *he is already on the way*. All that he is doing in providence and grace is a preparation for his coming. All the events of human history, all the great decisions of his august majesty whereby he ruleth all things—all these are tending towards the day of his appearing. Do not think that he delays his coming, and then upon a sudden he will rush hither in hot haste. He has arranged for it to take place as soon as wisdom allows. We know not what may make the present delay imperative; but the Lord knows, and that suffices. You grow uneasy because near two thousand years have passed since his ascension, and Jesus has not yet come; but you do not know what had to be arranged for, and how far the lapse of time was absolutely necessary for the Lord's designs. Those are no little matters which have filled up the great pause: the intervening centuries have teemed with wonders. A thousand things may have been necessary in heaven itself ere the consummation of all things could be arrived at. When our Lord comes it shall be seen that he came as quickly as he could, speaking after the manner of his infinite wisdom; for he cannot behave himself otherwise than wisely, perfectly, divinely. He cannot be moved by fear or passion so as to act hastily as you and I too often do. He dwells in the leisure of eternity, and in the serenity of omnipotence. He has not to measure out days, and months, and years, and to accomplish so much in such a space or else leave his life-work undone; but according to the power of an endless life he proceeds steadily on, and to him a thousand years are but as one day. Therefore be assured that the Lord is even now coming. He is making everything tend that way. All things are working towards that grand climax. At this moment, and every moment since he went away, the Lord Jesus has been coming back again. "Behold, he cometh!" He is on the way! He is nearer every hour!

And we are told that *his coming will be attended by a peculiar sign*. "Behold, he cometh *with clouds*." We shall have no need to question whether it is the Son of man who has come, or whether he is indeed come. This is to be no secret matter: his coming will be as manifest as yonder clouds. In the wilderness the presence of Jehovah was known by a visible pillar of cloud by day, and an equally visible pillar of fire by night. That pillar of cloud was the sure token that the Lord was in his holy place, dwelling between the cherubim. Such is the token of the coming of the Lord Christ.

> *Every eye the cloud shall scan,*
> *Ensign of the Son of man.*

So it is written, "And then shall appear the sign of the Son of man in heaven: and then shall all the tribes of the earth mourn, and they shall see the Son of man coming in the clouds of heaven with power and great glory." I cannot quote at this time all those many passages of Scripture in which it is indicated that our Lord will come either sitting upon a cloud, or "with the clouds," or "with the clouds of heaven;" but such expressions are abundant. Is it not to show that his coming will be *majestic?* He maketh the clouds his chariots. He cometh with hosts of attendants, and these of a nobler sort than earthly monarchs can summon to do them homage. With clouds of angels, cherubim and seraphim, and all the armies of heaven he comes. With all the forces of nature, thunder-cloud and blackness of tempest, the Lord of all makes his triumphant entrance to judge the world. The clouds are the dust of his feet in that dread day of battle when he shall ease him of his adversaries, shaking them out of the earth with his thunder, and consuming them with the devouring flame of his lightning. All heaven shall gather with its utmost pomp to the great appearing of the Lord, and all the terrible grandeur of nature shall then be seen at its full. Not as the Man of sorrows, despised and rejected of men, shall Jesus come; but as Jehovah came upon Sinai in the midst of thick clouds and a terrible darkness, so shall he come, whose coming shall be the final judgment.

The clouds are meant to set forth the *might*, as well as the majesty, of his coming. "Ascribe ye strength unto God: his excellency is over Israel, and his strength is in the clouds." This was the royal token given by Daniel the prophet in his seventh chapter, at the thirteenth verse, "I saw in the night visions, and, behold, one like the Son of man came with the clouds of heaven." Not less than divine is the glory of the Son of God, who once had not where to lay his head. The sublimest objects in nature shall most fitly minister to the manifest glory of the returning King of men. "Behold, he cometh;" not with the swaddling-bands of his infancy, the weariness of his man-hood, the shame of his death, but with all the glorious tapestry of heaven's high chambers. The hanging of the divine throne-room shall aid his state.

The clouds, also, denote *the terror of his coming to the ungodly*. His saints shall be caught up together with him in the clouds, to meet the Lord in the air; but to those that shall remain on earth the clouds shall turn their blackness and horror of dark-ness. Then shall the impenitent behold this dread vision—the Son of man coming in the clouds of heaven. The clouds shall fill them with dread, and the dread shall be abundantly justified,

94

for those clouds are big with vengeance, and shall burst in judgment on their heads. His great white throne, though it be bright and lustrous with hope to his people, will with its very brightness and whiteness of immaculate justice strike dead the hopes of all those who trusted that they might live in sin and yet go unpunished. "Behold, he cometh. He cometh with clouds."

I am in happy circumstances, because my subject requires no effort of imagination from me. To indulge fancy on such a theme would be a wretched profanation of so sublime a subject, which in its own simplicity should come home to all hearts. Think clearly for a moment, till the meaning becomes real to you. Jesus Christ is coming, coming in unwonted splendour. When he comes he will be enthroned far above the attacks of his enemies, the persecutions of the godless, and the sneers of sceptics. He is coming in the clouds of heaven, and we shall be among the witnesses of his appearing. Let us dwell upon this truth.

Our second observation is this: OUR LORD'S COMING WILL BE SEEN OF ALL. "Behold, he cometh with clouds, *and every eye shall see him, and they also which pierced him.*"

I gather from this expression, first, that *it will be a literal appearing, and an actual sight.* If the second advent was to be a spiritual manifestation, to be perceived by the minds of men, the phraseology would be, "Every mind shall perceive him." But it is not so: we read, "Every eye shall see him." Now, the mind can behold the spiritual, but the eye can only see that which is distinctly material and visible. The Lord Jesus Christ will not come spiritually, for in that sense he is always here; but he will come really and substantially, for every eye shall see him, even those unspiritual eyes which gazed on him with hate, and pierced him. Go not away and dream, and say to yourself, "Oh, there is some spiritual meaning about all this." Do not destroy the teaching of the Holy Ghost by the idea that there will be a spiritual manifestation of the Christ of God, but that a literal appearing is out of the question. That would be altering the record. The Lord Jesus shall come to earth a second time as literally as he has come a first time. The same Christ who ate a piece of a broiled fish and of a honeycomb after he had risen from the dead; the same who said, "Handle me, and see; for a spirit hath not flesh and bones, as ye see me have"

—this same Jesus, with a material body, is to come in the clouds of heaven. In the same manner as he went up he shall come down. He shall be literally seen. The words cannot be honestly read in any other way.

"Every eye shall see him." Yes, I do literally expect to see my Lord Jesus with these eyes of mine, even as that saint expected who long ago fell asleep, believing that though the worms devoured his body, yet in his flesh he should see God, whom his eyes should see for himself, and not another. There will be a real resurrection of the body, though the moderns doubt it: such a resurrection that we shall see Jesus with our own eyes. We shall not find ourselves in a shadowy, dreamy land of floating fictions, where we may perceive, but cannot see. We shall not be airy nothings, mysterious, vague, impalpable; but we shall literally see our glorious Lord, whose appearing will be no phantom show, or shadow dance. Never day more real than the day of judgment; never sight more true than the Son of man upon the throne of his glory. Will you take this statement home, that you may feel the force of it? We are getting too far away from facts nowadays, and too much into the realm of myths and notions. "Every eye shall see him," in this there shall be no delusion.

Note well that *he is to be seen of all kinds of living men:* every eye shall see him: the king and the peasant, the most learned and the most ignorant. Those that were blind before shall see when he appears. I remember a man born blind who loved our Lord most intensely, and he was wont to glory in this, that his eyes had been reserved for his Lord. Said he, "The first whom I shall ever see will be the Lord Jesus Christ. The first sight that greets my newly-opened eyes will be the Son of man in his glory." There is great comfort in this to all who are now unable to behold the sun. Since "every eye shall see him," you also shall see the King in his beauty. Small pleasure is this to eyes that are full of filthiness and pride: you care not for this sight, and yet you must see it whether you please or do not please. You have hitherto shut your eyes to good things, but when Jesus comes you *must* see him. All that dwell upon the face of the earth, if not at the same moment, yet with the same certainty, shall behold the once crucified Lord. They will not be able to hide themselves, nor to hide him from their eyes.

They will dread the sight, but it will come upon them, even as the sun shines on the thief who delights in the darkness. They will be obliged to own in dismay that they behold the Son of man: they will be so overwhelmed with the sight that there will be no denying it.

He will be seen of those who have been long since dead. What a sight that will be for Judas, and for Pilate, and for Caiaphas, and for Herod! What a sight it will be for those who, in their lifetime, said that there was no Saviour, and no need of one; or that Jesus was a mere man, and that his blood was not a propitiation for sin! Those that scoffed and reviled him have long since died, but they shall all rise again, and rise to this heritage among the rest—that they shall see him whom they blasphemed sitting in the clouds of heaven. Prisoners are troubled at the sight of the judge. The trumpet of assize brings no music to the ears of criminals. But thou must hear it, O impenitent sinner! Even in thy grave thou must hear the voice of the Son of God, and live, and come forth from the tomb, to receive the things done in thy body, whether they were good or bad. Death cannot hide thee, nor the vault conceal thee, nor rottenness and corruption deliver thee. Thou art bound to see in thy body the Lord who will judge both thee and thy fellows.

It is mentioned here that *he will especially be seen by those that pierced him*. In this is included all the company that nailed him to the tree, with those that took the spear and made the gash in his side; indeed, all that had a hand in his cruel crucifixion. It includes all of these, but it comprehends many more besides. "They also who pierced him" are by no means a few. Who have pierced him? Why those that once professed to love him, and have gone back to the world. Those that once ran well, "What did hinder them?" And now they use their tongues to speak against the Christ whom once they professed to love. They also have pierced him whose inconsistent lives have brought dishonour upon the sacred name of Jesus. They also have pierced him, who refused his love, stifled their consciences, and refused his rebukes. Alas, that so many of you should be piercing him now by your base neglect of his salvation! They that went every Sunday to hear of him, and that remained hearers only, destroying their own souls rather than yield to his infinite love: these pierced his tender heart. I wish I could plead effectually with you now, so that you would not continue any longer among the number of those that pierced him. If you will look at Jesus now, and mourn for your sin, he will put your sin away; and then you will not be ashamed to see him in that day. Even though you did pierce him, you will be able to sing, "Unto him that loved us, and washed us from our sins in his own blood." But, remember, if you persevere in piercing him, and fighting against him, you will still have to see him in that day, to your terror and despair. He will be seen by you and by me, however ill we may behave. And what horror will that sight cost us!

We never know how soon we may be cut off, and then we are gone for ever from the opportunity of benefiting our fellow-men. It were a pity to be taken away with one opportunity of doing good unused. So would I earnestly plead with you under the shadow of this great truth: I would urge you to make ready, since we shall both behold the Lord in the day of his appearing. Yes, I shall stand in that great throng. You also will be there. How will you feel? You are not accustomed, perhaps, to attend a place of worship; but you will be there, and the spot will be very solemn to you. You may absent yourself from the assemblies of the saints, but you will not be able to absent yourself from the gathering of that day. You will be there, one in that great multitude; and you will see Jesus the Lord as truly as if you were the only person before him, and he will look upon you as certainly as if you were the only one that was summoned to his bar.

Will you kindly think of all this as I close this second head? Silently repeat to yourself the words, "Every eye shall see him, and they also that pierced him."

And now I must close with the third head, which is a painful one, but needs to be enlarged upon: HIS COMING WILL CAUSE GREAT SORROW. What does the text say about his coming? "All kindreds of the earth shall wail because of him."

"All kindreds of the earth." Then *this sorrow will be very general*. You thought, perhaps, that when Christ came, he would come to a glad world, welcoming him with song and music. You thought that there might be a few ungodly persons who would be destroyed with the breath of his mouth, but that the bulk of mankind would receive him with delight. See how different—"All kindreds of the earth," that is, all sorts of men that belong to the earth; all earth-born men, men out of all nations and kindreds and tongues shall weep and wail, and gnash their teeth at his coming. This is a sad outlook! We have no smooth things to prophesy. What think you of this?

And, next, *this sorrow will be very great*. They shall "*wail*." I cannot put into English the full meaning of that most expressive word. Sound it at length, and it conveys its own meaning. It is as when men wring their hands and burst out into a loud cry; or as when eastern women, in their anguish, rend their garments, and lift up their voices with the most mournful notes. All the "kindreds of the earth shall wail": wail as a mother laments over her dead child; wail as a man might wail who found himself hopelessly imprisoned and doomed to die. Such will be the hopeless grief of all the kindreds of the earth at the sight of Christ in the clouds: if they remain impenitent, they shall not be able to be silent; they shall not be able to repress or conceal their anguish, but they shall wail, or openly give vent to their horror. What a sound that will be which will go up before high heaven when Jesus sits upon the cloud, and in the fulness of his power summons them to judgment! Then "they shall wail because of him."

Will your voice be heard in that wailing? Will your heart be breaking in that general dismay? How will you escape? If you are one of the kindreds of the earth, and remain impenitent, you will wail with the rest of them. Unless you now fly to Christ, and hide yourself in him, and so become one of the kindred of heaven, one of his chosen and blood-washed ones—who shall praise his name for washing them from their sins—unless you do this, there will be wailing at the judgment-seat of Christ, and you will be in it.

Then it is quite clear that men will not be universally converted when Christ comes; because, if they were so, they would not wail. Then they would lift up the cry, "Welcome, welcome, Son of God!" The coming of Christ would be as the hymn puts it—

> *Hark, those bursts of acclamation!*
> *Hark, those loud triumphant chords!*
> *Jesus takes the highest station.*
> *Oh, what joy the sight affords!*

These acclamations come from his people. But according to the text the multitude of mankind will weep and wail, and therefore they will not be among his people. Do not, therefore, look for salvation to some coming day, but believe in Jesus now, and find in him your Saviour at once. If you joy in him now, you shall much more rejoice in him in that day; but if you will have cause to wail at his coming, it will be well to wail at once.

Note one more truth. It is quite certain that when Jesus comes in those latter days *men will not be expecting great things of him.* You know the talk they have nowadays about "a larger hope." To-day they deceive the people with the idle dream of repentance and restoration after death, a fiction unsupported by the least tittle of Scripture. If these "kindreds of the earth" expected that when Christ would come they would all die out and cease to be, they would rejoice that thereby they escaped the wrath of God. Would not each unbeliever say, "It were a consummation devoutly to be wished"? If they thought that at his coming there would be a universal restoration and a general jail delivery of souls long shut up in prison, would they wail? If Jesus could be supposed to come to proclaim a general restoration they would not wail, but shout for joy. Ah, no! It is because his coming to the impenitent is black with blank despair that they will wail because of him. If his first coming does not give you eternal life, his second coming will not. If you do not hide in his wounds when he comes as your Saviour, there will be no hiding place for you when he comes as your Judge. They will weep and wail because, having rejected the Lord Jesus, they have turned their backs on the last possibility of hope.

Why do they wail *because of him?* Will it not be because they will see him in his glory, and they will recollect that they slighted and despised him? They will see him come to judge them, and they will remember that once he stood at their door with mercy in his hands and said, "Open to me," but they would not admit him. They refused his blood: they refused his righteousness: they trifled with his sacred name; and now they must give an account for this wickedness. They put him away in scorn, and now, when he comes, they find that they can trifle with him no longer. The days of child's-play and of foolish delay are over; and now they have solemnly to give in their life's account. See, the books are opened! They are covered with dismay as they remember their sins, and know that they are written down by a faithful pen. They must give an account; and unwashed and unforgiven they cannot render that account without knowing that the sentence will be, "Depart, ye cursed." This is why they weep and wail because of him.

O souls, my natural love of ease makes me wish that I could preach pleasant things to you; but they are not in my commission. I need scarce wish, however, to preach a soft gospel, for so many are already doing it to your cost. As I love your immortal souls, I dare not flatter you. As I shall have to answer for it in the last great day, I must tell you the truth.

> *Ye sinners seek his face*
> *Whose wrath ye cannot bear.*

Seek the mercy of God now. I have come here in pain to implore you to be reconciled to God. "Kiss the Son lest he be angry, and ye perish from the way, when his wrath is kindled but a little. Blessed are all they that put their trust in him" (Ps. 2: 12).

But if you will not have my Lord Jesus, he comes all the same for that. He is on the road now, and when he comes you will wail because of him. Oh that you would make him your friend, and then meet him with joy! Why will ye die? He gives life to all those who trust him. Believe, and live.

8

THE STAR AND THE WISE MEN

"Now when Jesus was born in Bethlehem of Judea in the days of Herod the king, behold, there came wise men from the east to Jerusalem, saying, Where is he that is born King of the Jews? for we have seen his star in the east, and are come to worship him.

When they had heard the king, they departed; and, lo, the star, which they saw in the east, went before them, till it came and stood over where the young child was. When they saw the star, they rejoiced with exceeding great joy."—Matt. 2 : 1, 2, 9, 10.

SEE the glory of our Lord Jesus Christ, even in his state of humiliation! He is born of lowly parents, laid in a manger and wrapped in swaddling bands; but, lo! the principalities and powers in the heavenly places are in commotion. First, one angel descends to proclaim the advent of the new-born King, and suddenly there is with him a multitude of the heavenly host singing glory unto God. Nor was the commotion confined to the spirits above; for in the heavens which overhang this earth there is a stir. A star is deputed on behalf of all the stars, as if he were the envoy and plenipotentiary of all worlds to represent them before their King. This star is put in commission to wait upon the Lord, to be his herald to men afar off, his usher to conduct them to his Presence, and his body-guard to sentinel his Cradle.

Earth, too, is stirred. Shepherds have come to pay the homage of simple-minded ones: with all love and joy they bow before the mysterious child; and after them from afar come the choice and flower of their generation, the most studious minds of the age. Making a long and difficult journey, they too at last arrive, the representatives of the Gentiles. Lo! the kings of Seba and Sheba offer gifts—gold, frankincense, and myrrh. Wise men, the leaders of their peoples, bow down before him, and pay homage to the Son of God. Wherever Christ is he is honourable. "Unto you that believe he is honour." In the day of small things, when the cause of God is denied entertainment, and is hidden away with things which are despised, it is still most glorious. Christ, though a child, is still King of kings; though among the oxen, he is still distinguished by his star.

If wise men of old came to Jesus and worshipped, should not we come also? My intense desire is that we all may pay homage to him of whom we sing, "Unto us a child is born; unto us a son is given." Let those of us who have long worshipped worship anew with yet lowlier reverence and intenser love. And God grant—oh, that he would grant it!—that some who are far off from him spiritually, as the Magi were far off locally, may come to-day and ask, "Where is he that is born King of the Jews? for we have come to worship him." May feet that have been accustomed to broad roads, but unaccustomed to the narrow path, this day pursue that way till they see Jesus, and bow before him with all their hearts, finding salvation in him. These wise men came naturally, traversing the desert; let us come spiritually, leaving our sins. These were guided by the sight of a star; let us be guided by faith in the divine Spirit, by the teaching of his word and all those blessed lights which the Lord uses to conduct men to himself. Only let us come to Jesus. It was well to come unto the babe Jesus, led by the feeble beams of a star; you shall find it still more blessed to come to him now that he is exalted in the highest heavens, and by his own light reveals his own perfect glory. Delay not, for this day he cries, "Come unto me, all ye that labour and are heavy laden, and I will give you rest" (Matt. 10:28).

Let us try to do three things. First, let us *gather light from this star;* secondly, let us *gather wisdom from these wise men;* and thirdly, let us *act as wise men helped by our own particular star*.

First, then, LET US GATHER LIGHT FROM THIS STAR. May the Spirit of the Lord enable us so to do.

I suppose you have each one his own imagination as to what this star was. It would seem to have been altogether supernatural, and not a star, or a comet of the ordinary kind. It was not a constellation, nor a singular conjunction of planets: there is nothing in the Scriptures to support such a conjecture. In all probability it was not a star in the sense in which we now speak of stars: for we find that it moved before the wise men, then suddenly disappeared, and again shone forth to move before them. It could not have been a star in the upper spheres like others, for such movements would not have been possible. Some have supposed that the wise men went in the direction in which the star shone forth in the heavens, and followed the changes of its position: but it could not in that case have been said that it stood over the place where the young child was. If the star was at its zenith over Bethlehem, it would have been in its zenith over Jerusalem too; for the distance is so small that it would not have been possible to observe any difference in the position of the star in the two places.

It must have been a star occupying quite another sphere from that in which the planets revolve. We believe it to have been a luminous appearance in mid-air; probably akin to that which led the children of Israel through the wilderness, which was a cloud by day and a pillar of fire by night. Whether it was seen in the daylight or not we cannot tell. Chrysostom and the early fathers are wonderfully positive about many things which Scripture leaves in doubt, but as these eminent divines drew upon their imagination for their facts, we are not under bonds to follow them. They aver that this star was so bright as to be visible all day long. If so, we can imagine the wise men travelling day and night; but if it could be seen only by night, the picture before us grows far more singular and weird-like as we see these easterns quietly pursuing their star-lit way, resting *perforce* when the sun was up, but noiselessly hurrying at night through slumbering lands. These questions are not of much importance to us, and therefore we will not dwell long upon them.

Only here is a first lesson: *if it should ever be that men should fail to preach the Gospel, God can conduct souls to his Son by a star*. Ah! say not only by a star, but by a stone, a bird, a blade of grass, a drop of dew.

> *Remember that Omnipotence*
> *Has servants everywhere.*

Therefore, despond not when you hear that one minister has ceased to preach the Gospel, or that another is fighting against the vital truth of God. Their apostasy shall be to their own loss rather than to the hurt of Jesus and his church; and, sad though it be to see the lamps of the sanctuary put out, yet God is not dependent upon human lights, he is the Shekinah light of his own holy place. Mortal tongues, if they refuse to preach his word, shall have their places supplied by books in the running brooks and sermons in stones. The beam shall cry out of the wall, and the timber shall answer it. When chief priests and scribes have all gone out of the way, the Lord puts stars into commission, and once more in very deed the heavens are telling the glory of God, and the firmament is showing his handiwork. Sooner than lack speakers for the incarnate God, mountains and hills shall learn eloquence and break forth into testimony. Jehovah's message shall be made known to the utmost ends of the earth. God shall save his own elect; he shall give to Christ to see of the travail of his soul and to be satisfied. His counsel shall stand, and he will do all his pleasure. Hallelujah!

Now, when the Lord does use a star to be his minister, what is the order of his ministry? We may learn by this enquiry what kind of ministry God would have ours to be if we are stars in his right hand. We also shine as lights in the world: let us see how to do it.

We notice, first, that star-preaching is *all about Christ*. We do not know what the colour of the star was, nor the shape of the star, nor to what magnitude it had attained; these items are not recorded, but what is recorded is of much more importance: the wise men said: "We have seen *his* star." Then the star which the Lord will use to lead men to Jesus must be Christ's own star. The faithful minister, like this star, belongs to Christ; he is Christ's own man in the most emphatic sense. Before we can expect to be made a blessing, we must ourselves be blessed of the Lord. If we would cause others to belong to Jesus, we must belong wholly to Jesus ourselves. Every beam in that star shone forth for Jesus. It was *his* star, always, and only, and altogether. It shone not for itself, but only as *his* star: as such it was known and spoken of—"we have seen his star." As I have already said, there is no note taken of any peculiarity that it had except this one, that it was the star of the King. I wish that you and I, whatever our eccentricities or personalities may be, may never make so much of them as to attract men's attention to them. May people never dwell upon our attainments or our deficiencies, but may they always observe this one thing, that we are men of God, that we are ambassadors of Christ, that we are Christ's servants, and do not attempt to shine for ourselves, or to make ourselves conspicuous; but that we labour to shine for him, that his way may be known upon earth, his saving health among all people.

It is well for us to forget ourselves in our message, to sink ourselves in our Master. We know the names of several of the stars, yet they may each one envy that star which remains anonymous, but can never be forgotten because men who sought the King of Israel knew it as "*his* star." Though you be but a very little star, twinkling for Jesus; however feeble your light may be, be it plain that you are *his* star, so that if men wonder *what* you are, they may never wonder whose you are, for on your very forefront it shall be written, "Whose I am and whom I serve." God will not lead men to Christ by us unless we are Christ's heartily, wholly, unreservedly. In his temple our Lord uses no borrowed vessels; every bowl before the altar must be his own. It is not consistent with the glory of God for him to use borrowed vessels. He is not so poor as to come to that. This lesson is worthy of all acceptation. Are you in a hurry to preach, young man? Are you sure you are Christ's? Do you think it must be a fine thing to hold a company of people listening to your words? Have you looked at it in another light? Have you weighed the responsibility of having to speak as Christ would have you speak, and of yielding yourself in your entire personality to the utterance of the mind of God? You must be consecrated and concentrated if you hope to be used of the Lord. If you have one ray, or ten thousand rays, all must shine with the one design of guiding men to Jesus. You have nothing now to do with any object, subject, design, or endeavour, but Jesus only: in him, and for him, and to him must you live henceforth, or you will never be chosen of the Lord to conduct either wise men or babes to Jesus. See ye well to it that perfect consecration be yours.

Note, next, that true star-preaching *leads to Christ*. The star was Christ's star itself, but it also led others to Christ. It did this very much because it moved in that direction. It is a sad thing when a preacher is like a sign-post pointing the way but never following it on his own account. Such were those chief priests at Jerusalem: they could tell where Christ was born, but they never went to worship him; they were indifferent altogether to him and to his birth. The star that leads to Christ must always be going to Christ. Men are far better drawn by example than driven by exhortation. Personal piety alone can be owned of God to the production of piety in others. "Go," say you: but they will not go. Say "come," and lead the way: then they will come. Do not the sheep follow the shepherd? He who would lead others to Christ should go before them himself, having his face towards his Master, his eyes towards his Master, his steps towards his Master, his heart towards his Master. We are so to live that we may without boasting exhort those around us to have us for an example. Oh, that all who think themselves to be stars would themselves diligently move towards the Lord Jesus. The star in the east led wise men to Christ because it went that way itself: there is a wisdom in example which truly wise men are quick to perceive. This star had such an influence upon the chosen men that they could not but follow it: it charmed them across the desert. Such a charm may reside in you and in me, and we may exercise a powerful ministry over many hearts, being to them as loadstones, drawing them to the Lord Jesus.

Happy privilege! We would not merely show the road, but induce our neighbours to enter upon it. We read of one of old, not that they told him of Jesus, but that "they brought him to Jesus." We are not only to tell the story of the Cross, but we are to persuade men to fly to the Crucified One for salvation. Did not the king in the parable say to his servants, "Compel them to come in"? Assuredly he girds his own messengers with such a compelling power that men cannot hold out any longer, but must follow their lead and bow at the King's feet. The star did not draw, "as it were with a cart rope," nor by any force, material and physical; yet it drew these wise men from the remote east right to the manger of the new-born Child. And so, though we have no arm of the law to help us, nor patronage, nor pomp of eloquence, nor parade of learning, yet we have a spiritual power by which we draw to Jesus thousands who are our joy and crown.

The man sent of God comes forth from the divine presence

permeated with a power which makes men turn to the Saviour and live. Oh! that such power might go forth from all God's ministers, yea, from all God's servants engaged in street-preaching, in Sunday Schools, in tract-visitation, and in every form of holy service. God uses those whose aim and intent it is to draw men to Christ. He puts his Spirit into them, by which Spirit they are helped to set forth the Lord Jesus as so lovely and desirable that men run to him and accept his glorious salvation. It is a small thing to shine, but it is a great thing to draw. Any cast-away may be brilliant; but only the real saint will be attractive for Jesus. I would not pray to be an orator, but I do pray to be a soul-winner. Do not aim at anything short of leading men to Jesus. Do not be satisfied to lead them to orthodox doctrine, or merely to bring them to a belief in those views which you hold to be Scriptural, valuable as that may be. It is to the Person of the incarnate God that we must bring them: to his feet we must conduct them that they may worship him: our mission is not accomplished, it is a total failure, unless we conduct our hearers to the house where Jesus dwells, and then stand over them, keeping watch over their souls for Jesus' sake.

Once more, the star which God used in this case was a star that *stopped at Jesus:* it went before the wise men till it brought them to Jesus, and then it stood still over the place where the young child was. I admire the manner of this star. There are remarkable stars in the theological sky at the present time: they have led men to Jesus, so they say, and now they lead them into regions beyond, of yet undeveloped thought. The gospel of the Puritans is "old-fashioned"; these men have discovered that it is unsuitable for the enlarged intellects of the times; and so these stars would guide us further still. To this order of wandering stars I do not belong myself, and I trust I never shall. Progress beyond the Gospel I have no desire for. "God forbid that I should glory save in the cross of our Lord Jesus Christ" (Gal. 6: 14). When the star had come to the place where the young child was, it stood still: and so should the gracious mind become settled, fixed, immovable. The wise men knew where to find that star, and where to find the young child by it: so be it with us. Oh, you that have hitherto been diligent in leading souls to Christ, never indulge for a single moment the notion that you need a broader philosophy or a deeper spirituality than are to be found in Jesus. Abide in him. Cry, "O God, my heart is fixed; my heart is fixed."

There is nothing beyond Christ which is worth a moment's thought. Do not lose your paradise in Christ for another taste of that tree of knowledge-of-good-and-evil which ruined our first parents. Stick you to the old points: your one subject Christ, your one object to bring men to Christ, your one glory the glory of Christ. Standing by your Lord, and there alone, from this day to the last day, you will secure a happy, honoured and holy life. They said of Greece after her fall that it had become so ruined that you might search for Greece in Greece and fail to find it: I fear I must say that some professed preachers of the gospel have roamed so far away from it that you cannot find the gospel in their gospel, nor Christ himself in the Christ they preach. So far have some diverged from the grand essential soul-saving truth beyond which no man ought to dare to think of going, that they retain nothing of Christianity but the name. All that is beyond truth is a lie; anything beyond revelation is at best a minor matter, and most probably is an old wives' fable, even though he may be of the masculine gender who invented it. Stand you to your colours, you who hope to be used of the Lord. Abide so that men shall find you in twenty years' time shining for Jesus and pointing to the place where the Saviour is to be found, even as you are doing now. Let Jesus Christ be your ultimatum. Your work is done when you bring souls to Jesus, and help to keep them there, by being yourself "steadfast, unmovable." Be not carried away from the hope of your calling; but hold fast even the form of sound words, for it may be that in letting go the form you may lose the substance also.

Now that we have somewhat rejoiced in the light of the star, let us see if we can GATHER WISDOM FROM THE WISE MEN. Perhaps you have heard the "much speaking" of tradition as to who they were, whence they came, and how they travelled. In the Greek church, I believe, they know their number, their names, the character of their retinue, and what kind of ornaments were on their dromedaries' necks. Details which are not found in the word of God you may believe or not, at your pleasure, and you will be wise if your pleasure is not to believe too much. We only know that they were Magi, wise men from the East, possibly of the old Parsee religion, watchers if not worshippers of the stars. We will not speculate about them, but learn from them.

They did not content themselves with admiring the star and comparing it with other stars, and taking notes as to the exact date of its appearance, and how many times it twinkled, and when it moved, and all that; but *they practically used the teaching of the star.* Many are hearers and admirers of God's servants, but they are not wise enough to make fit and proper use of the preaching. They notice the peculiarity of the preacher's language, how much he is like one divine, how much he is unlike another; whether he coughs too often or speaks too much in his throat; whether he is too loud or too low; whether he has not a provincial tone, whether there may not be about him a commonness of speech approaching to vulgarity; or, on the other hand, whether he may not be too florid in his diction. Such fooleries as these are the constant observations of men for whose souls we labour. They are perishing, and yet toying with such small matters.

With many it is all they go to the house of God for: to criticise in this paltry fashion. I have even seen them come to this place with opera glasses, as if they came hither to inspect an actor who lived and laboured to amuse their leisure hours. Such is the sport of fools; but these were wise men, and therefore practical men. They did not become star-gazers and stop at the point of admiring the remarkable star; but they said, "Where is he that is born King of the Jews? for we have seen his star in the east, and are come to worship him." They set out at once to find the new-born King, of whose coming the star was the signal. Oh, how I wish that you were all wise in this same manner! I would sooner preach the dullest sermon that was ever preached than preach the most brilliant that was ever spoken if I could by that poor sermon lead you quite away from myself to seek the Lord Jesus Christ. That is the one thing I care about. Will you never gratify me by enquiring after my Lord and Master? I long to hear you say, "What is the man talking about? He speaks about a Saviour; we will have that Saviour for ourselves. He talks about pardon through the blood of Christ; he speaks about God coming down among men to save them; we will find out if there is any reality in this pardon, any truth in this salvation. We will seek Jesus and find for ourselves the blessings which are reported to be laid up in him." If I heard you all saying this I should be ready to die of joy.

Is not this a good day on which to set out to find your Saviour? Some of you that have postponed it long, would it not be well to set out at once ere this expiring year has seen its last day? These wise men appear to have set out as soon as they discovered the star: they were not among those who have time to waste in needless delays. "There is the star," said they; "away we go beneath its guidance. We are not satisfied with a star, we go to find the King whose star it is!" And so they set out to find Christ immediately and resolutely.

Being wise men, *they persevered in their search after him.* We cannot tell how far they journeyed. Travelling was extremely difficult in those times. There were hostile tribes to avoid, the broad rivers of the Tigris and the Euphrates to cross, and trackless deserts to penetrate; but they made nothing of difficulty or danger. They set out for Jerusalem, and to Jerusalem they came, seeking the King of the Jews. If it be true that God has taken upon himself our nature, we ought to resolve to find him, let it cost what it may. If we must circumnavigate the globe to find a Saviour, the distance and the expense ought to be nothing so long as we may but reach him. Were the Christ in the bowels of the earth, or in the heights of heaven we ought not to rest till we come at him. Everything that was necessary for their expedition the wise men soon gathered together, regardless of expense; and off they went following the star that they might discover the Prince of the kings of the earth.

At length they came to Jerusalem, and here new trials awaited them. It must have been a great trouble to them when they asked, "Where is he that is born King of the Jews?" and the people shook their heads as if they thought the question an idle one. Neither rich nor poor in the metropolitan city knew anything of Israel's King. The ribald multitude replied, "Herod is king of the Jews. Mind how you speak of another king, or your head may have to answer for it. The tyrant brooks no rival." The wise men must have been more astonished still when they found that Herod was troubled. They were glad to think that he was born who was to usher in the age of gold; but

Herod's face grew blacker than ever at the bare mention of a king of the Jews. His eyes flashed, and a thunder-cloud was upon his brow; a dark deed of murder will come of it, though for the moment he conceals his malice. There is tumult all through the streets of Jerusalem, for no man knows what grim Herod may do now that he has been roused by the question, "Where is he that is born King of the Jews?" Thus there was a ferment in Jerusalem, beginning at the palace; but this did not deter the wise men from their search for the promised Prince. They did not pack up their bales and go back and say, "It is useless to try to discover this questionable personage who is unknown even in the country of which he is King, and who appears to be terribly unwelcome to those who are to be his subjects. We must leave to another day the solution of the question: "Where is he that is born King of the Jews?"

These earnest-minded seekers were not dispirited by the clergy and the learned men when they came together. To the chief priests and scribes the question was put, and they answered the enquiry as to where Christ would be born, but not a mother's son among them would go with the wise men to find this new-born King. Strange apathy! Alas, how common! Those who should have been leaders were no leaders; they would not even be followers of that which is good, for they had no heart towards Christ. The wise men rose superior to this serious discouragement. If the clergy would not help them they would go to Jesus by themselves. Oh, if you are wise you will say, "I will find Christ alone if none will join me: if I dig to the centre, I will find him; if I fly to the sun, I will find him; if all men put me off, I will find him; if the ministers of the gospel appear indifferent to me, I will find him: the kingdom of heaven of old suffered violence, and the violent took it by force, and so will I." The first Christians had to leave all the authorized teachers of the day behind, and to come out by themselves: it will be no strange thing if you should have to do the same. Happy will it be if you are determined to go through floods and flames to find Christ; for he will be found of you. Thus these men were wise because, having started on the search, they persevered in it till they found the Lord and worshipped him.

Notice that they were wise because, when they again saw the star, "they rejoiced with exceeding great joy." While enquiring among the priests at Jerusalem they were perplexed, but when the star shone out again, they were at ease and full of joy: this joy they expressed, so that the evangelist recorded it. In these days very wise people think it necessary to repress all emotion, and appear like men of stone or ice. No matter what happens, they are stoical, and raised far above the enthusiasm of the vulgar. It is wonderful how fashions change, and folly stands for philosophy. But these wise men were children enough to be glad when their perplexity was over, and the clear light shone forth. It is a good sign when a man is not ashamed to be happy because he hears a plain, unmistakable testimony for the Lord Jesus. It is good to see the great man come down from his pedestal, and, like a little child, rejoice to hear the simple story of the Cross. Give me the hearer who looks not for fineries, but cries out, "Lead me to Jesus. I want a guide to Jesus, and nothing else will suit me." Why, truly, if men did but know the value of things they would rejoice more to see a preacher of the gospel than a king. If the feet of the heralds of salvation be blessed, how much more their tongues when they tell out the tidings of a Saviour. These wise men, with all their mystic learning, were not ashamed to rejoice because a little star lent them its beams to conduct them to Jesus. We unite with them in rejoicing over a clear Gospel ministry. For us all else is darkness, sorrow, and vexation of spirit; but that which leads us to our own glorious Lord is spirit, and light, and life. Better the sun should not shine than that a clear Gospel should not be preached. We reckon that a country flourishes or decays according as Gospel light is revealed or withdrawn.

Now follow these wise men a little further. They have come to the house where the young child is. What will they do? Will they stand looking at the star? No: *they enter in.* The star stands still, but they are not afraid to lose its radiance, and behold the Sun of righteousness. They did not cry, "We see the star, and that is enough for us; we have followed the star, and it is all we need to do." Not at all. They lift the latch, and enter the lowly residence of the babe. They see the star no longer, and they have no need to see it, for there is he that is born King of the Jews. Now the true Light has shone upon them from the face of the child; they behold the incarnate God. Oh how wise you will be if, when you have been led to Christ by any man, you do not rest in his leadership, but must see Christ for yourselves. How much I long that you may enter into the fellowship of the mystery, pass through the door, and come and behold the young child, and bow before him. Our woe is that so many are so unwise. We are only their guides, but they are apt to make us their end. We point the way, but they do not follow the road; they stand gazing upon us. The star is gone; it did its work, and passed away: Jesus remains, and the wise men live in him. Will any of you be so foolish as to think only of the dying preacher, and forget the ever-living Saviour? Come, be wise, and hasten to your Lord at once.

These men were wise, last of all—and I commend their example to you—because when they saw the child *they worshipped*. Theirs was not curiosity gratified, but devotion exercised. We, too, must worship the Saviour, or we shall never be saved by him. He has not come to put away our sins, and yet to leave us ungodly and self-willed. Oh you that have never worshipped the Christ of God, may you be led to do so at once! He is God over all, blessed for ever, adore him! Was God ever seen in such a worshipful form before? Will you not worship God when he thus comes down to you and becomes your brother, born for your salvation? Here nature itself suggests worship: Oh, may grace produce it! Let us hasten to worship where shepherds and wise men and angels have led the way.

Here let my sermon come to a pause even as the star did. Enter the house and worship! Forget the preacher. Let the starlight shine for other eyes. Jesus was born that you might be born again. He lived that you might live. He died that you might die to sin. He is risen, and to-day he maketh intercession for transgressors that they may be reconciled to God through him. Come, then; believe, trust, rejoice, adore! If you have neither gold, frankincense, nor myrrh, bring your faith, your love, your repentance, and falling down before the Son of God pay him the reverence of your hearts.

And now I turn to my third and last point, which is this: LET US ACT AS WISE MEN UNDER THE LIGHT OF OUR STAR. We too have received light to lead us to the Saviour: I might say that for us many stars have shone to that blessed end. I will, however, on this point content myself with asking questions.

Do you not think that there is some light for you in your particular vocation, some call from God in your calling? Listen to me, and then listen to God. These men were watchers of the stars; therefore a star was used to call them. Certain other men soon after were fishermen, and by means of an amazing take of fish the Lord Jesus made them aware of his superior power, and then he called them to become fishers of men. For a star-gazer a star; for a fisherman a fish. The Master-Fisher hath a bait for each one of his elect, and oftentimes he selects a point in their own calling to be the barb of the hook. Were you busy yesterday at your counter? Did you hear no voice saying "Buy the truth and sell it not"? When you closed the shop last night did you not bethink yourself that soon you must close it for the last time? Do you make bread? and do you never ask yourself, "Has my soul eaten the bread of heaven?" Are you a farmer? do you till the soil? Has God never spoken to you by those furrowed fields and these changing seasons, and made you wish that your heart might be tilled and sown? Listen! God is speaking! How I wish that your common vocation would be viewed by you as concealing within itself the door to your high vocation. Oh that the Holy Spirit would turn your favourite pursuits into opportunities for his gracious work upon you.

I wish that those of you who conclude that your calling could never draw you to Christ would make a point of seeing whether it might not be so. We are to learn from ants, and swallows, and cranes, and conies; surely we need never be short of tutors. It did seem that a star was an unlikely thing to head a procession of eastern sages, and yet it was the best guide that could be found; and so it may seem that your trade is an unlikely thing to bring you to Jesus, and yet the Lord may so use it. There may be a message from the Lord to thee in many a left-handed providence; a voice for wisdom may come to thee from the mouth of an ass; a call to a holy life may startle thee from a bush, a warning may flash upon thee from a wall, or a vision may impress thee in the silence of night when deep sleep falleth upon men. Only be thou ready to hear and God will find a way of speaking to thee. Answer the question as the wise men would have answered it, and say, "Yes, in our calling there is a call to Christ."

Then, again, *what should you and I do better in this life than seek after Christ?* The wise men thought all other pursuits of small account compared with this. "Who is going to attend to that observatory and watch the rest of the stars?" They shake their heads, and say they do not know: these things must wait; they have seen *his* star, and they are going to worship him. But who will attend to their wives and families, and all besides, while they make this long journey? They reply that every lesser thing must be subordinate to the highest thing. Matters must be taken in proportion, and the search after the King of the Jews, who is the desire of all nations, is so out of all proportion great that all the rest must go. Are not you, also, wise enough to judge in this sensible fashion? If you were to take a week, and give it wholly to your own soul, and to seeking Christ, would it not be well spent? How can you live with your soul in jeopardy? Oh that you would say, "I must get this matter right; it is an all-important business, and I must see it secure." This would be no more than common-sense. If you are driving, and a trace is broken, do you not stop the horse, and set the harness right? How, then, can you go on with the chariot of life when all its harness is out of order, and a fall means eternal ruin? If you will stop driving to arrange a buckle for fear of accident, I would beg of you to stop anything and everything to see to the safety of your soul.

See how the engineer looks to the safety-valve: are you content to run more desperate risks? If your house were not insured, and you carried on a hazardous trade, the probability is you would feel extremely anxious until you had arranged that matter: but your soul is uninsured, and it may burn for ever; will you not give heed to it? I beseech you be just to yourself; be kind to yourself. Oh! see to your eternal well-being.

When we do come near to Jesus, let us ask ourselves this question, "*Do we see more in Jesus than other people do?*" for if we do, we are God's elect, taught of God, illuminated by his Spirit. We read in the Scriptures that when these wise men saw the young child they fell down and worshipped him. Other people might have come in and seen the child, and said, "Many children are as interesting as this poor woman's babe." Ay, but as these men looked, they saw: all eyes are not so blessed. Eyes that see are gifts from the All-seeing One. Carnal eyes are blind; but these men saw the Infinite in the infant; the Godhead gleaming through the manhood; the glory hiding beneath the swaddling bands. Undoubtedly there was a spiritual splendour about this matchless Child! We read that Moses' father and mother saw that he was a "goodly child"; they saw he was "fair unto God," says the original. But when these elect men saw that holy thing which is called the Son of the Highest, they discovered in him a glory all unknown before. Then was his star in the ascendant to them: he became their all in all, and they worshipped with all their hearts. Have you discovered such glory in Christ? "Oh!" says one, "you are always harping upon Christ and his glory. You are a man of one idea!" Precisely so. My one idea is that he is "altogether lovely," and that there is nothing out of heaven nor in heaven that can be compared with him even in his lowest and weakest estate. Have you ever seen as much as that in Jesus? If so, you are the Lord's; go you, and rejoice in him. If not, pray God to open your eyes until, like the wise men, you see and worship.

Lastly, learn from these wise men that when they worshipped they did not permit it to be a mere empty-handed adoration. Ask yourself, *"What shall I render unto the Lord?"* Bowing before the young Child, they offered "gold, frankincense and myrrh," the best of metals and the best of spices; an offering to the King of gold; an offering to the priest of frankincense; an offering to the child of myrrh. Wise men are liberal men. Consecration is the best education. To-day it is thought to be wise to be always receiving; but the Saviour said, "It is more blessed to give than to receive." God judges our hearts by that which spontaneously comes from them: hence the sweet cane bought with money is acceptable to him when given freely. He doth not tax his saints or weary them with incense; but he delights to see in them that true love which cannot express itself in mere words, but must use gold and myrrh, works of love and deeds of self-denial, to be the emblems of its gratitude. You will never get into the heart of happiness till you become unselfish and generous; you have but chewed the husks of religion which are often bitter, you have never eaten of the sweet kernel until you have felt the love of God constraining you to make sacrifice.

9

THE RIGHT OBSERVANCE OF THE LORD'S SUPPER

"For I have received of the Lord that which also I delivered unto you, That the Lord Jesus the same night in which he was betrayed took bread: and when he had given thanks, he brake it, and said, Take, eat: this is my body, which is broken for you: this do in remembrance of me. After the same manner also he took the cup, when he had supped, saying, This cup is the new testament in my blood: this do ye, as oft as ye drink it, in remembrance of me. For as often as ye eat this bread, and drink this cup, ye do shew the Lord's death till he come." 1 Cor. 11: 23–26.

WE have no respect whatever for the ordinances of men in religion. Anything that is only invented by churches, or councils, is nothing whatever to us. We know of two ordinances instituted by the Lord Jesus Christ, the baptism of believers and the Lord's supper; and we utterly abhor and reject all pretended sacraments of every kind. And because we observe these two ordinances, and these two only, we are the more concerned that they should be properly used, and duly understood, and that they should minister to the edification of those who participate in them. We would have those who are baptized understand what is meant by that expressive rite, that they, being dead with Christ, should also be buried with him, and rise with him into newness of life. And when we observe the Lord's supper, we feel a deep and earnest desire that none should come to the table in ignorance of the signification of the observance,—or that, at least, ignorance may not be an occasion of eating unworthily; but that we may comprehend what we are doing, and understand the spiritual meaning of this pictorial instruction by which the Lord Jesus Christ would, even until the end of the age, remind his Church of his great sacrifice upon the Cross.

So, first, I will speak briefly concerning THE FORM OF THE LORD'S SUPPER.

We do not think that it is at all material where that supper is held. It is just as valid and helpful in your own private apartments, in your bedroom, or in your parlour, as it is in any place where Christians usually congregate. We do not attach so much importance as some people do to the time when it is observed; but we are astonished that High Churchmen should be opposed to evening communion, for, if any definite time for partaking of it can be quoted from Scripture, it certainly is the evening. I should like to ask the Ritualists whether they can find any instance, either in holy or profane things, of a supper being eaten before breakfast, until they invented that absurd practice. There is no time that is more like the first occasion when the Master celebrated the ordinance with his disciples than is the evening of the day. Then it was that he gathered the twelve apostles together, and instituted this blessed memorial feast. At Emmaus, too, it was at the close of the day that he was made known to his two disciples in the breaking of bread. It must be sheer superstition, utterly unwarranted by Holy Scripture, which tells us that the Lord's *supper* can only be properly received *in the morning*, and that we ought not to eat anything before we partake of the sacred emblems! We reject all such nonsense, for we find no authority for it in the only standard which we recognize, that is, the inspired Word of God. Let us see what it teaches us concerning this ordinance.

We learn, first, that *the Lord's supper should begin with thanksgiving.* So the Master himself evidently commenced it: "He took bread and gave thanks." All through the supper, the emotion of gratitude should be in active exercise. It is intended that we should give thanks for the bread, at the same time giving still more emphatic thanks for the sacred body which it represents. Then we should also give thanks for the cup, and for that most precious blood which is therein represented to us. We cannot rightly observe the Lord's supper unless we come to the table, blessing, praising, magnifying, and adoring our Saviour, praising him even for instituting such a festival of remembrance, such a memorial ordinance to help our frail memories; and praising him yet more for giving us so blessed a thing to remember as his own great sacrifice for our sin.

After the thanksgiving, it is very clear that our Divine Lord *broke the bread*. We scarcely know what kind of bread was used on that occasion; it was probably the thin passover cake of the Jews; but there is nothing said in Scripture about the use of leavened or unleavened bread, and therefore it matters not which we use. Where there is no ordinance, there is no obligation; and we are, therefore, left free to use the bread which it is our custom to eat. When the Master had broken the bread, *he gave it to his disciples*, and said, "Take, eat;" and they all participated in eating it. And this, mark you, is essential to the right observance of the Lord's supper; so that, when the priest, in celebrating mass, takes the wafer, which is not bread, and which he does not break, but which he himself eats whole, there is no Lord's supper there. Whatever it may be called, it is not the Lord's supper. In the eating of the bread, there must be the participation of such a number of faithful, godly disciples of Christ as may be present, or else it is not the ordinance which the Lord instituted.

That being done, the next thing was that, "*After the same manner also he took the cup;*" that is to say, after the same manner of thanksgiving, blessing God for the fruit of the vine, which was henceforth to be the emblem of his poured-out blood. Even so should we do. It is no vain thing to praise the Lord, though we do it twice, thrice; ay, and ten thousand times. Well did the Psalmist say, "Praise ye the Lord: for it is good to sing praises unto our God; for it is pleasant; and praise is comely" (Ps. 147: 1). Specially comely is it for us to praise our God when we are calling to remembrance the unspeakable gift of his only-begotten and well-beloved Son.

Then came the partaking of the cup,—the fruit of the vine,—of which the Master expressly said, "Drink ye all of it." Hence, when the Church of Rome takes away the cup from the people, and denies it to them, there is no observance of the Lord's supper, for another essential part of the ordinance is left out. It may be the mass, or it may be anything else; but it is not the supper of the Lord. There must be a participation by all the faithful in the cup, as well as in the bread.

Further, in order that this may be the Lord's supper in very truth, *it must be observed in remembrance of Christ*, who said to his disciples, "This do in remembrance of me." From which we learn that only those who know him much come to his table, for how shall we remember what we never knew? And how shall we remember him with whom we have never spoken, and in whom we have never believed? You are not to come to the Lord's supper to get faith; you must have faith first, or else you have no right to draw nigh to this sacred spot. What do ye here? If you suppose that this is a saving ordinance, I must say to you what Christ said to the Sadducees, "Ye do err, not knowing the scriptures" (Matt. 22 : 29). Salvation comes to us through faith in our Lord Jesus Christ, and it is the result of the effectual working of the Spirit of God within us. This supper is a most instructive ordinance for those who are saved; but those who are not born again, and are not, by grace, members of the Lord's family, have no right here. They who ate the passover were such as were born in the priest's house, or bought with the priest's money; and if you have been born in Christ's house, or bought with Christ's blood, if you know, by blessed experience, the meaning of regeneration and redemption, then may you come to the communion table. But, if not, as the passover was only intended for Israel, so is this supper a family feast for those who belong to Jesus Christ, and no others may come to it; if they do come, it will be at the peril of eating and drinking unworthily, since they are unable to discern the Lord's body.

I have thus given you a very brief account of the form of observing the Lord's supper, as we find it in the New Testament. You notice that I have not said anything about a chalice, or a paten, or about consecrating the elements, or uplifting the host, and all that Romish rubbish of which some people think so much. The reason for my silence is that there is nothing about these things in the Bible. "To the law, and to the testimony: if they speak not according to this word, it is because there is no light in them." Clear away all the additions of superstition, they are but the dust and the rust which have accumulated during the ages, and they spoil and mar the purity of Christ's own ordinance.

Now, secondly, from our text, I gather THE IMPORTANCE OF THE LORD'S SUPPER.

First, *because it was revealed by the Lord himself.* Paul wrote to the Corinthians, "I have received of the Lord that which also I delivered unto you." Matthew, Mark, Luke, and John were all accessible to Paul; and, though they had not then written their Gospels, yet he could have learnt from them how the Saviour instituted the supper. But, as if Christ would not let it be second-hand, he was pleased to declare to Paul personally —to Paul himself, directly and distinctly—how the supper should be celebrated. The apostle says, "I have received of the Lord," not "*we*", not "I and the rest of the apostles and disciples," but "*I* have received of the Lord," indicating a definite personal revelation from Christ as to this matter. After the Lord Jesus had gone up into his glory, his revelations were but few; yet this was one of them. He would have his disciples, therefore, pay due attention to this important matter which he thus specially revealed to Paul.

I have already referred to the next point, but it is so important that I remind you again that *this supper was commanded by the Lord.* He said, "This do in remembrance of me;" and again, "This do ye, as oft as ye drink it, in remembrance of me." If I love Christ, I am bound to keep his commandments; and among the rest of his commandments, this one in which he here says, "This do." I might have thought, from the conduct of some professing Christians, that Jesus must have said, "This *do not*"; but as he said, "This do ye," where shall I find an apology for those who either never have done it at all, or, being his people, do it so seldom that he could not say to them, "This do ye, as *oft* as ye drink it," but he might rather say, "This do ye as *seldom* as ye drink it," since the idea of frequency does not enter into their observance of it? But what Christ revealed and commanded, it is incumbent upon his own beloved ones to obey.

Notice, again, that *this supper was instituted by Christ himself, and he himself first set the example for its observance.* As to baptism, you remember how he said, "Thus it becometh us to fulfil all righteousness," and so he set us the example in that matter; and, in the supper, it was he who first blessed and brake the bread, it was he who first passed the cup, and said, "This cup is the new covenant in my blood." If he had given the command, and the apostles had been the first to attend to it, it would have been binding upon us; but, inasmuch as, in addition to giving the command concerning it, he himself set the example of observing it, sitting at the centre of the table, with the twelve all around him, I think he has put a special halo about this ordinance, and we must by no means forget, or neglect, or despise it.

Remember, too, that *he established it on a very special occasion.* To my mind, it is very touching to read, "The Lord Jesus the same night in which he was betrayed took bread." I cannot help noticing that the apostle is very particular to say here, "The Lord Jesus." Very often, he uses the name "Christ" in speaking of the Saviour; but here it is, "the Lord Jesus," to show the awe and reverence which the apostle felt as, by faith, he saw the Master at the first communion table. Paul could not forget that, though Jesus was then Lord of all, he was that same night betrayed. He that ate bread with him, lifted up his heel against him, and sold him for thirty pieces of silver; yet, even while the anticipation of that betrayal, and all which it involved, was tearing his heart asunder, he remembered us, and established this ordinance that, by refreshing our memories concerning his blessed self, we might not be left to play the traitor, too, but might be kept steadfast in every time of trial. It seems to me that we must be specially careful to observe such an ordinance as this, instituted when our Saviour's heart was breaking with anguish on our behalf!

And do remember, too, the importance of the ordinance, because of *the peculiar personal motive with which it was instituted:* "This do in remembrance" of what? Of Christianity, and its doctrines and practices? No, but, "in remembrance of ME." You know how tenderly a thing comes home to you if a dying husband says, "This do, my beloved one, in remembrance of me, when I am dead and gone." You never fail to do that, I am sure, if it is in your power. You know how it is with a friend, who has gone from you, and who has left you some forget-me-not. You treasure it with the utmost care; the memento is very precious for your friend's sake; and our dear Lord and Master has put about this supper all the loveliness of his personality, all the graciousness of his affection for us, and all the tenderness that ought to be in our love to him. If there is anything that he bids you do, you ought to do it; but, when it is something to be done in remembrance of him, you must do it; your love impels you to do it. Are you not ashamed if you are not doing it in the most loving, humble, grateful, and earnest manner possible, as becomes the memory of him who loved you, and gave himself for you? I should not like to urge any Christian to come to the communion table; I feel as if I would do nothing to spoil the perfect spontaneity of it. If you do not love him, do not come to his table; but if you do love him, come because you love him; come because you remember him, and because you wish to be helped to remember him yet more.

There is one more thing which adds to the importance of this supper; and that is, *it is to be observed "till he come."* It is not an ordinance, then, for the first Christian centuries alone, to be, as it were, the bridge between the ceremonialism of the Old Testament and the spirituality of the New Testament. No; it is intended to be celebrated "till he come." We must keep on gathering at his table, giving thanks, breaking bread, and proclaiming his death, till the trump of the archangel shall startle us, and then we shall feel it to be truly blessed to be found obediently remembering him when he puts in his appearance at the last. As he comes to us, we shall say, "Blessed Master, we have done as thou didst bid us; we have kept alive thy memory in the world, to ourselves, and to those who looked on as we broke the bread, and drank of the cup, in thy name, and now we rejoice to see thee in thy glory." I do not know that the meeting between Christ and his people could happen at a better time than if he were to come when they were gathered at his table, obeying his command, and showing his death "till he come."

But now, thirdly, let us enquire, IN WHAT SPIRIT OUGHT WE TO COME TO THIS TABLE?

I should say, first, that we are bound to come in the spirit of *deep humility*. To my mind, it is a very humbling thing that we should need anything to help us to remember Christ. I see no better evidence of the fact that we are not yet perfectly sanctified, for, if we were, we should need nothing to help us to remember him. There is, alas, still an imperfection in our memory; and that, strangest and saddest thing of all, in respect to Jesus himself. It is extraordinary that we should ever require anything to help us to remember him. Can he, to whom we owe so much, be ever forgotten by us? The fact that this ordinance is to be observed, in remembrance of him "till he come," is a humbling proof that, till that glorious event, his people's memories will be faulty, and they will need this double forget-me-not to remind them of him who is their All-in-all.

What do I see on that table? I see bread there. Then I gather this humbling lesson, that I cannot even keep myself in spiritual food. I am such a pauper, such an utter beggar, that my own table cannot furnish me with what I want, and I must come to the Lord's table, and I must receive, through him, the spiritual nutriment which my soul requires. What do I see in the cup? I see the wine which is the token of his shed blood; what does that say to me but that I still need cleansing? Oh, how I rejoice in that blessed text in John's first Epistle: "If we walk in the light, as he is in the light, we have fellowship one with another"! And then what follows? That we do not need to make any more confession of sin, because we are quite cleansed from it? Nothing of the sort; "and the blood of Jesus Christ his Son cleanseth us from all sin." We still need the cleansing fountain even when we are walking in the light, as God is in the light; and we need to come to it every day. And what a mercy it is that the emblem sets forth the constant provision of purifying blood whereby we may be continually cleansed!

But, next, we must come *very thankfully*. Some pull a long face when they think about coming to the communion table; like Mrs. Toogood, who is described in Rowland Hill's *Village Dialogues*. She made a mistake about the week that the ordinance was to be observed, so she did not play cards during that week, and kept herself wonderfully pure, poor old soul; and then, when she found, on the Sunday, that she had made a blunder as to the time, she said she had wasted the whole week in getting ready! I hope we do not know anything of that method of keeping the sacred feast; we are to come in a very different frame of mind from that, for we are not coming to a funeral supper, but to the luxuries and dainties that become a marriage feast. Let us come, therefore, with thankfulness, as we say to one another concerning our Lord, "He is not here, for he is risen, glory be to his holy name!" These tokens of remembrance tell us that he has gone where it was expedient for him to go, that the Holy Spirit might descend upon us. Therefore, rejoice even because of the absence of your Lord, for it is well that he should be gone up into the glory. And, as we come to the table, each one feeling what a sinner he is, how unworthy he is to come, how unfit he is to sit with saints, should not each heart say, "Bless the Lord, O my soul: and all that is within me, bless his holy name"?

But, certainly, we should come to the table *with great thoughtfulness*. There are some, we are told, who do not discern the Lord's body; let us think and pray, lest we should be numbered with them. If there be no right thinking, there will be no true spiritual feeling, and there will be no Lord's supper so far as you are concerned. Think of what your Saviour suffered for you, what he has done for you, and what he has gone to prepare for you. Let us remember that the bread sets forth the suffering of his body, that the wine typifies the blood of the atonement whereby we are cleansed, that the two apart, the body separated from the blood, form a most suggestive symbol of the matchless death whereby we are made to live. Think much at the table, but think of nothing but Christ.

But come, also, *with great receptiveness*. It is a meal, you know; we receive the bread and the wine. So, come to the table begging the Lord to give you the grace to feed upon himself spiritually, that you may, by faith, receive him into your inward parts; that, in your inmost soul, you may have the virtue of his life and of his death. Come empty, therefore; for so you will be the better qualified to feed upon him. Come hungering and thirsting; thus you will have the greater appetite for Christ.

Now I finish my discourse by dwelling, for a minute or two, UPON THE GREAT LESSONS WHICH THIS SUPPER INCIDENTALLY TEACHES.

The first lesson is, that *Jesus is for us*. There has been a great dispute over this verse, "This is my body, which is broken for you." The word "broken" appears in some of the ancient manuscripts; but it is, undoubtedly, an interpolation. It is absent from several of those manuscripts upon which we are obliged to rely for the correct text of the New Testament; and, hence, very properly, the Revised Version reads, "This is my body, which is for you." And, to my mind, that rendering gives a new thought which is well worth having. "This is my body, which is for you." That is to say, Christ is for you; does not the supper itself say that? The bread represents his body for you; the wine represents his blood for you. We know that it is for you, because you are going to eat it. There is nothing that is more certainly a man's than what he eats or drinks; and, in like manner, when we have really received Christ by faith, there is no possibility of robbing us of him. "This is my body, which is for you." Oh, what a blessed doctrine! Lay hold of this great truth, all that there is in Christ is for you. All the fulness of the Godhead is in him, "and of his fulness have all we received, and grace for grace" (John 1: 16).

The next lesson is, that *his blood has sealed the covenant.* "This cup is the new covenant in my blood." There was a covenant that cursed us, the covenant of works. There is another covenant that has blessed the elect of God, and shall bless them to all eternity, the covenant of grace; and this covenant is signed, and sealed, and ratified, in all things ordered well; and for its seal it has the blood of God's own Son. Therefore it shall stand fast for ever and ever. So, as you partake of that cup, drink with joy, because it reminds you that God hath made with you "an everlasting covenant ordered in all things and sure."

The third great doctrine that is taught by this supper is that *believers feed on Christ himself.* Sometimes they forget this, and they try to feed on doctrines. They will make as great a mistake as if the Jew, when he went up to the tabernacle, had tried to feed on the curtains, or the altar, or the golden tongs. What did he have for food? Why, the peace-offering! When he drew near to his God, he fed on the sacrifice; and the true food of a believer is Christ Jesus himself. We can do it, and we must do it, spiritually, by having our hearts and our minds resting upon what Christ is, and what he has done, and so feeding upon our Lord Jesus Christ.

I have finished when I have mentioned one more lesson which is to be learned from this ordinance. It is clear, from this supper, that *the way to remember Christ is to feed on him again and again.* Is it not a strange thing that, if I have had a great mercy, the way to recollect that mercy is to come to God, and get another mercy? If Christ was ever sweet to my taste, the way to perpetuate that sweetness is to come and taste him again. Do not try to live upon your old experiences. Even the best kind of bread will not keep very long; it soon gets musty if you lay it by. You need to have bread constantly coming fresh from the oven. Even the manna, which came down from heaven, could not be kept, lest it should breed worms; and it is so with the food for your souls.